Frank D. Rogers

Folk-Stories of the Northern Border

Frank D. Rogers

Folk-Stories of the Northern Border

ISBN/EAN: 9783744779524

Printed in Europe, USA, Canada, Australia, Japan

Cover: Foto ©ninafisch / pixelio.de

More available books at **www.hansebooks.com**

Folk-Stories of the Northern Border

—BY—

FRANK D. ROGERS.

1907
THOUSAND ISLANDS PUBLISHING CO,
CLAYTON, N. Y

FOLK=STORIES.

FULLY ILLUSTRATED

FROM DRAWINGS BY

ROBERT H. ROGERS, UNION '99.

To the memory of
EDWARD C. ROGERS,
Whose untimely taking off by the very elements
he so much loved removes a brother and a
critic upon whose practical knowl-
eage of practical subjects the
author was wont to draw,
This work is affectionately dedicated.

Autobiography,	11
Preface,	14
Burial of Harry Millikin,	17
Perry's Victory, (Old Song)	23
The Dance at Johnny Beaver's,	25
A Cannon Shotted With Gold Coin,	31
The Legend of Calumet Island,	42
Daniel Millikin, American,	54
Wind and Weather Permitting,	63
Wars and Rumors of Wars,	71
Up the St. Lawrence, 1796,	132
Down the St. Lawrence, 1818,	138
Captivity of Mrs. Howe,	143
A Pioneer's Hardships,	154
Folk-Stories,	165
Three Links,	203
A Bit of Topography,	216
The French Settlers,	218
Two Old-Fashioned Boys,	229
The Last Haul,	269

Yours, truly,
Frank D. Rogers.

AUTOBIOGRAPHY.

The sponsor for this little volume has long been a contributor to the leading periodicals along the lines of romance as well as deep thought. But his contributions have been almost invariably returned, when the return postage was prepaid, accompanied by a printed note indicative of a wholesale business in declinations, "on the grounds that our columns are not adapted to its publication, but as early as a meeting of the directors can be held the policy of our magazine will be changed to meet the requirements of your production."

Clever, but positively deceitful managing editors! Thus ever has budding genius been stifled by sordid directors whose interest in the uplifting of humanity is confined to the office elevator.

The author was born on the North Prairie in the city of Chicago. True, he first opened his eyes a hundred miles westward from Lincoln Park, but the corporation lines have been so often extended that it is believed the place of his birth is at present within the city limits. He had barely attained the age of five years than immediately the civil war broke out with all its attendant carnage. Even at that tender age he was determined to enlist in his country's cause, and in fact was enrolled by a recruiting officer, but was recalled by parental restrictions. At six he was a successful pilot of runaway slaves on the Underground Railway, much to the discomfiture of the largest slave-holders, who had put a price on his head. At the age of ten years he removed to New York state bringing with him his parents, whom he succeeded in giving a good common school education the following summer. At fourteen he was yet undecided whether to practice medicine, be a blacksmith, join a circus, or run for congress. Haply the last rash choice was averted by his choosing a mercantile career, which he abandoned after breaking the firm by which he was employed in a little less than six months. He then adopted journalism, bought a newspaper which, however, another sold, but not until he had outdone Dr. Tanner's fast by eleven days, not exactly as an experiment but rather as a matter of necessity to which many editors uncomplainingly submit, the while writing menus for each day of the week. Later he went on the road, but finding expenses greater than the combined sales and collections, he concluded to develop new fields, and so took up life insurance. With his usual aptness for the new and novel, he succeeded in writing one risk, extra hazardous, upon himself and never caught another. Then he started a magazine which a subscriber stopped because he was appointed receiver. Then and not till then did this great government of politicians, by the lawyers, and for the spoils, demand of our hero his immediate and undivided attention at Washington. Thither he went to bolster up a frail and tottering dynasty. He had no sooner thrown himself into the breach than congress convened and laid out work for a succeeding congress by enacting new laws to be unmade at the next session. After deciphering the hieroglyphics which congressmen are pleased to call "writin'," correcting their bad spelling and worse grammar, he paralyzed the whole governmental fabric by resigning. "Not dead, but resigned," they said of him, and he was sought by many and pointed out as one who had the nerve to cut loose from governmental dugs and face a blank and uncertain future upon his own resources.

After having been connected with so many defunct enterprises it was but natural that he should give his attention to an apprenticeship with an undertaker, one who laughs when others are in dead earnest, and straightens out a patient after the doctors give him up.

PREFACE.

The making of a book is accomplished in many ways. In this particular instance the last chapter was written first. Then at odd times other chapters were written, and as the work progressed it received something like systematic attention. The subject-matter is one in which the writer has ever taken a delightful intesest. It is a pleasure to write of the triumphs and record the trials constantly recurring in the simple affairs of our forefathers whose heroic endurance made and saved our nation. They it was who made possible the astounding progress of this nineteenth century.

The foundation of these stories of every day heroism is mainly from the lips of a paternal grand-mother whose simple though impressive language kindled an admiration for a people whose oftimes most heroic acts the historian has passed as unworthy of record in the face of warlike deeds. That the privation and suffering, toil and combat patiently borne by the struggling pioneers, who in their unpretentious ways silently, and yet with irresistible energy, paved the way to prosperity for successive generations, shall be the more keenly realized may be after all the purpose of putting a dress on these unpublished Folk-Stories of the Northern Border.

To make the stories appear continuous the same characters have been employed, and that with a care to their individuality in the incidents narrated. Inconsistencies of time will be discovered by keen readers who, noting the customs portrayed, may discover the generation in which the material facts sprang into existence.

The world is slow to recognize the every-day heroism on

the farm, in the kitchen or at the desk. Nevertheless it is there, and often the sacrifices made in the daily discharge of simple duty amounts to a heroism worthy the pen of a Bancroft.

Burns saw poetry in a frightened mouse and a broken daisy. A limping hare attracted his sympathetic pen. Shakspeare writes of sheep-shearing and greenwood shades. Scott, Byron and Pope turn the brilliancy of their genius upon the daily affairs of men and there is a revelation as of the electric search-light. The Bible itself abounds in the daily heroism of peoples of humble calling. Longfellow, Bryant, Whittier, Emerson, Lowell, and the whole galaxy of American stars are not above the heroism of the humble walks of life. Ian Maclaren has immortalized Logiealmond, the "Drumtochy" of his sketches, by his depictions of the homely Scotch life that existed in that community years ago, and our own New England life has latterly received some attention on that line. Not an old town in existence but would furnish abundant material for the story writer after the historian, scorning the precious dust and ore rich with pleasing memories, has departed with the nuggets.

Pictures of home life! Paintings of the true-hearted, honest poor! Go read "Beside the Bonny Brier Bush;" go see and hear Denman Thompson in "The Old Homestead," and say whether it is author and actor, or the portrayal of the unsullied lives of a true people, unknown to deceit and guile, that reaches the heart and starts the tear unbidden.

Folk-Stories had their existence in fact. They are not imagination or romance, but have a real existence in the unrecorded annals of the American settlers of the St. Lawrence River and Lake Ontario regions, once popularly known as the Black River country.

Burial of Harry Millikin.

When the appointed hour for the funeral arrived the neighbors and friends had gathered from the North and South shores, from the islands and points, and from the settlement recently founded at the head of the creek. The men were grouped about the little clearing in front of the cabin, and inside the womenfolk busied themselves at nothing, or sat listlessly holding their hands in their laps. In subdued tones they discussed the incidents of the very few funerals they had attended "back east," and many an eye moistened and many a breath shortened as the thought of friends and associations severed by death and separation was brought the more vividly to mind by the mournful surroundings. The minister, a good old Presbyterian man, arrived on horseback a full hour late, but the delay caused neither surprise nor vexatious comment, for funerals were not conducted in a hurry nor with military precision in those days. The cabin was about 12 feet by 16 inside, with front and rear doors opening into the principal room on opposite sides. To the right of the front entrance stood a bed in a recess, its white valance of bleached cotton attracting much attention for the richness of the decoration. Blue

cambric curtains, parted in the center and tied back with red
braid completed the arrangement, except a linen coverlid, out
of which the bedposts grew to the ceiling, and ending in a
cherry knob. Next beyond the recess was a narrow stairway,
and beyond that and taking up the corner was the thorn in
the side of less favored housewives, a regular pantry with
shelves. The remainder of the house below was at once kitchen,
dining room and parlor, the fireplace and oven forming a respectable annex, and opening conveniently into the side to the
left.

On a pine table covered with an unfinished piece of linen
lay the coffin, a crude affair made by old Hank Tubbs, the
cooper. It was fashioned out of pine boards, with but one an-
gle in the sides, and stained a dirty black. The lid was cham-
fered with a plane so as to leave a streak of natural wood
around its edge. The handles once were black, but having
seen long service on a tool chest they could lay no claim to
the merit of newness. A few shavings had been strewn on the
bottom, by request, as even that show of comfort was not customary. The rough interior was not relieved by so much as
a bit of lace for it was believed that such "fixin's" were not
only a waste of material but a downright sin as well. The
emaciated form of Harry lay flat upon his back, mouth open,
eyes staring at the bare joist overhead, and his arms and hands
laid straight down his sides with the fingers spread in a con-
vulsive grasp. That the sight was one that would terrify the
most strong can not be denied, but it must be remembered
that the undertaker's art had not reached the ideal at that day.

The minister took a position at the head of the coffin
whence he issued orders earnestly and with the sternness of a
newly appointed brigadier-general. The few relatives, besides
the parents, filed down from the garret and were seated about

the coffin on planks supported by blocks of wood. A rigid observance of the order of relationship was maintained, the cousins coming in last. Indeed no little commotion and a slight delay was caused by a third cousin who unwittingly seated herself in front of a second cousin of her father.

The good man read the most of Deuteronomy, then turned back to Genesis and read and expounded for a good half hour. Then he started off on a long prayer which was of the most liberal character, geographically speaking. He had passed Europe, Asia, and the other continents, the government officials, who were not nearly so much in need of it as in later years, and was excusing the failures of the Whigs, when a clock, half as tall as a man, set up a most frightful striking. At first it started off soberly to do business in the regulation manner, but no sooner had it discharged that duty than it was seized with a frenzy for striking. It pounded off fifty and was merrily hurrying along toward the hundred mark when the good dominie, who had gradually raised his voice so as to be heard above the whir and clatter of the presumptuous, not to say irreligious timepiece, peremptorily shouted in sheer desperation:

"Stop the clock!"

And then appealingly—

"Will some one stop the clock, please?"

For a moment no movement was made in compliance. Then Tim Fagan sprang up, overturning a stool in his haste, and seizing the clock by weights, hands and pendulum, as if to choke it to death, restored quiet and the good man resumed. After the man at the clock had kept his grip on the offender for what seemed to him almost an entire day, he gradually released his hold, backed carefully away and sat down—on the floor where his stool had been. The fall startled everybody,

and all but stopped the preacher. The shock was transmitted
to the wall, thence to the clock, which, with an ominous growl
began to announce the flight of time on the twenty-four hour
system, and finished the hundredth stroke just as the exasper-
ated Tim wrenched it from its moorings and flung it high out
in the wood pile.

The prayer was followed by some remarks, after which
the march to the log schoolhouse was taken up. The coffin lid
which had been standing against the wall, a horrid silhouette
against the whitewashed sheathing, was now fastened to its
place by nails driven part way down so as to afford easy withdrawal. Then the burden was raised to the shoulders of four
as badly frightened boys as ever saw a corpse for the first time,
and borne to a cart to which was attached a pair of oxen. Slowly the procession wound over the irregular course to the log
building where the master held school in winter. There the
coffin was deposited upon a table in the center of the room, the
men taking one side and the women the other. For two mor-
tal hours the preacher dwelt upon the moral impossibility of
young Harry's attaining a home with the blest, and empha-
sized the discourse with such lurid word-pictures of his satanic
majesty's domain that the two Collins boys ran out screaming
when a dog crawled from an obscure corner. They believed
the evil one himself had come to verify the awful utterances
which had wrought up the entire congregation. Women sobbed,
children cried aloud, and men controlled their feelings by grim
efforts that were more painful than outright expression.

"You will never see your little Harry again," consolingly
shouted the divine, "You will put away his boots, his cap, his
skates and his sled—"

The father groaned aloud.

"You will have a vacant place at the table, and you will

ever think of the one that is gone when you assemble for each meal as the cold wind and snow—"

The mother shrieked.

"His young companions will miss him from the boyish games, from skating, swimming, fishing, hunting—"

The dog howled.

"I say again you will never see him in your midst for he will soon be laid away, food for worms and eventuate in dust."

A shudder passed over his hearers, but emboldened by his success the heartless man sought to bind up their aching wounds by a peroration on the doctrine of election.

"If poor little Harry is among the elect let us rejoice; but if he is not then are we again admonished of the awful fate in store for most all of us."

"Let the chorister line the hymn while I rest my throat before proceeding to that 'narrow house, a house of clay' to hold the final of these, to me, impressive services."

A choir of six voices with flute and bass viol accompaniment rendered Duke Street from music printed with "buckwheat notes." The congregation was commanded to "view the corpse." This done, each one felt in duty bound to remark, "How natteral he looks!" The procession was re-formed and slowly wound its way back to the Millikin clearing where a grave had been made. The coffin was lowered with ropes which sawed and rasped painfully as they were withdrawn, all but overturning it, so tenacious was the clay into which they were imbedded. There was no outside box, but in this instance a board was laid on the coffin to afford a slight protection from animals of the burrowing kind. Then each of the bearers in turn seized a spade and threw in a clod of earth which fell upon the coffin with an echoing thump that nearly broke the remaining heartstrings of the now thoroughly prostrate parents. The mourners and friends shook hands with the preacher, and as they turned away remarked in a distinctly audible aside, "How well the elder done!"

That worthy was heard to remark, after the ordeal, that he felt that he had "been of great comfort to them, because they wept copiously throughout the whole discourse."

*   *   *   *

Green grows the turf above Harry's grave, with not so much as a sod to mark his resting place. The field has been alternated with the crops of the farm, lo, these many years, and my informant, an old man, bent and gray, took me as near the spot as a memory faded by the cares of sixty and more years would direct.

"It was about here, or mayhap a leetle furder down, but the woods are gone and the fields so big I may be far astray from the spot. I was the next youngest of the bearers, and so long was I afeered to come anigh the spot I may have miscalculated."

Miscalculated! Reader it may not be so long until one may search in vain for your resting place and mine.

Perry's Victory.

Ye sons of Columbia give ear to my story
    Who fought with brave Perry where cannons did roar;
His valor has gained you an immortal glory,
    Which will last till Father Time shall be no more.

The tenth of September, I pray let's remember,
    As long as the globe on it's axis rolls round,
Our tars and marine upon Lake Erie were seen
    To make the proud flag of Great Britain come down

The van of our fleet the bold British did meet—
    Commanded by Perry the Lawrence bore down.
Our guns they did roar with such terrific power
    The savage Britons did tremble at the great sound.

The Lawrence sustained a most terrible fire;
    She fought three to one for two glasses or more.
Gallant Perry, undaunted, firmly stood by her
    While the proud foe heavy broadsides did pour.

Her masts are all shattered, her rigging all tattered,
    Her yards and her booms being all shot away;
But few left on the deck to manage the wreck,
    Our hero on board her no longer could stay.

Says Perry, "Those villains, they mean for to drown us,
  Push on my brave boys, you need never have fear."
Then he off with his coat and plugged up the boat
  And away through fire and smoke he did steer.

The famous Niagara, now proud of her Perry,
  Displayed all her banners in gallant array.
Twenty-five guns on her decks she did carry
  Which soon put an end to this bloody affray.

Brave Elliott, whose valor must now be recounted,
  On board the Niagara he well played his part.
His gallant assistance to Perry afforded
  Well placed him the second on Lake Erie's chart.

Hurrah for our flag! General Harrison, too!
  For Perry's bold fleet loud praised by all powers.
Hurrah for his message, may it ever prove true:
  "We have met the enemy—and they are ours."

The Dance at Johnny Beaver's.

"My name, hits John Baptiste Bivver. Ahm cum off Montrahall on raff, me. Ahm cum hire for feesh wid yous. Got for me one job?"

Yes, Collins would give him a hand-share.

"What dat you call handsheer?"

It was explained.

"Well, I get mebbe nothing, mebbe four tousand, me. Ahm lucky Bivver. Cum on go pullem seine rat off for make good cotch quite plain." (Easy.)

He was told it was too windy to cast out the nets.

"Yaas? Bimeby she blow some more. What-a-matter now? Me no 'fraid watter, Ahm cum off Montrahall, me. Ahm no peesoup Frencher. Ahm trappe vurry gross feesh by Montrahall."

"My fambly on dock. You got some shanty I live in for while?"

One end of the cooper shop was provided for him, and in the foregoing scraps of conversation he was formally installed factotum on the Collins fishing grounds.

Beaver was short, broad-shouldered and heavy-chested, active, and had a happy temperament. His cheek bones were high, eyes black, beard thin and in patches, arms short. Corduroys, moccasins, a pea jacket, a velvet toque on one side of his head, and a sash that once was red, gave him a rather jaunty appearance. His wife was a full-blooded white girl, superior to the life she must lead with him. She had married for better but could hardly have done worse had she looked beyond a bare living and the rearing of a large family.

La Famine made much of Johnny Beaver, while in turn he found much to almost reach the superlative in Montreal, the city to which he likened all events, all nature and all superstitions in the comparative degree.

Beaver dearly loved music and dancing. Hearing a fiddle in the hands of a fisherman he was seized with a desire to give a ball, and forthwith set about inviting all whom he met to come to his dance. A pack-peddler, a fish-peddler, who counted out fish as "forty-six, fifty-seven," thus gaining ten, and the new handsharers were alike bidden to come in his quaint vocabulary:

"Ahm goin' mek one donce on my house. Yous all cum. Twon't be le grande bal masque like I mek on Montrahall, but all mans and womans round cum on. I tek de bed down, turn stove 'roun'! Den yampytampy, yampytampy," and Johnny, a full grown man, bursting with exuberance, improvises a partner out of a broomstick, and executes the French four with more vigor than grace.

The stove, one of the elevated oven pattern, had been "turned around," and heated red. At the farther end of the shop a potash kettle was filled with live coals and set upon bricks. The remainder of the scant furniture was tossed out doors to make more room.

Johnny's guests began to arrive early, but many that were invited remained away. The host was in no wise grieved at the apparent slight for the reason that the absentees were

"THE FIDDLER WAS SEATED ON A SHAVING HORSE."

fully replaced by the arrival of an equal number who came without invitation. Among the latter were some young men who came just to see the fun, but forgot their purpose and joined merrily in the festive dance.

The fiddler was seated upon a shaving-horse, and that in turn was raised upon a couple of fish barrels. Three sets "formed on" and after alternately sawing the strings and twisting the pegs, the fiddler settled back and poured body, soul and arms into " The Lancers, " the while thumping with the sole of his right boot to the time of his music.

" Jine hands and circle ! "

Men in heavy boots, red shirts, and coatless, made the plank floor tremble at the word, and the human ring made a complete turn three bars ahead of the music, and had time to breathe before the next move was prompted.

" First four for'ard and back—alamand-de-left ! "

Right hands elevated and with left arm akimbo, palm outward, the figure is cut in a lively dance—no walking allowed —and the couples return to place once more to catch breath as the tardy music vigorously brings up the rear.

" Balance pard-ners—grand right and left ! "

A general grabbing of hands, right hand, left hand, anybody's hand, and return to place with ample time for those who have lost partners to make the proper exchange of positions. Two changes and a " breakdown " is the rule of the floor, and panting, laughing, chattering, the three sets vacate the floor which is quickly taken by those who did not " get into " the first sets.

Johnny is called " Mr. Beaver " so frequently as to cause him to imagine himself a member of parliament. He beams right and left upon his guests, and after much coaxing consents to do a clog which makes him indeed a hero. This done he announces supper in the following speech delivered from the shaving-horse temporarily vacated for the purpose by the string orchestra of one piece:

"Now, you'll mek ver' small racket while Ahm goin' hax yous for supper. Tain' ver' nice but hits de bes' what we didn't get and de smoke sturgeon is de bess meat dat swims except the crane I never tass it. Ahm smoke it myself where I learn donn Moatrahall Heat 'em all up and I ver' mooch tank yous for ten cent quite plain. Dats hall."

"Bung jour," he added by way of a polite finish to his remarks, and jumping to the floor he walked on his hands to the end of the room and came to his feet by turning a handspring. The clapping of hands and remarks of approval filled the simple-minded half-breed with joy unspeakable, and while preparations were made for lunch he gave an exhibition successively of the snake, green corn and canoe dances much to the disgust of his white wife who had never seen him make such an exhibition of savage customs. Her protests made him the merrier, and the encouragement given him by his guests led him to another prank. Seizing a hatchet he performed the scalp dance over the fiddler and raised that worthy's scalp a dozen times, ending the performance with a whoop and throwing the hatchet with such skill that it stuck fast in a pine post forming a part of the frame. Some of his guests were slightly alarmed at this feature of the entertainment, but it was forgotten when the music again started.

After lunch the dancing began in earnest. "Opera Reel," "Moneymusk," and "McDonald's Reel," were followed by an eight-hand reel.

Truthful compliments were exchanged, the music pronounced the best, and the lunch a feast, on this felicitous occasion. The only waltzers in the party were Nancy Mareeau and Joby Collins who had been sweethearts since infancy, it was declared. They had the floor to themselves for the third time when a gruff voice called from outside the partly open door:

"Nan!"

Nancy turned about and faced her father who had hurried across lots when his daughter was missed. Choking with rage he hoarsely growled:

"Nan, you drop that cur and come straight home!"

The excitement was evident, but suppressed. The fiddler rested, and Nancy plead:

"Oh, now, pa! Come in and waltz just once with me. Do come! Just once!" And the saucy girl waltzed alone to the door and held out a hand invitingly to the man whom no other, man or woman, dared cross when he was in anger.

"Don't be a fool, Nan," he said, half pleadingly, "come away and don't have nothink to say to a relative of old Hank Collins. You know who cut my seine, Nanny, 'twere old Hank and I never forgets."

"Oh! dam the seine, pa, if I must say it. You will hold a grudge the longest of any man! Come in now, daddy, and teach the boys to waltz. Come!

The old lion was tamed as usual when he shook his mane at his favorite child, and Nancy led him to the middle of the floor where they elicited general admiration in the graceful waltz to an old tune which the fiddler had amended by forgetting the last strain and improvising one of his own creation.

Nancy with her usual tact proposed to her father to go home and the old soldier and sailor, now fisherman, departed with his hands free from the blood of Joby Collins, contrary to his threat made at the outset.

Just at daylight the candles were snuffed out and a lively breakdown was danced as a finishing touch to the night's enjoyment. As they departed, one after another in the dawn, Johnny shook hands heartily and was heard to exclaim more than once:

"Ahm ver' mooch tanks for yous! Cum on my beeg house down Montrahall nex' summer, we donce tree day, tree night and have mans to blow de horn and mek de big' fid' go 'bum, bum,' an Ahm make yous acquaint' de mayor, and de counsel, and de halderman, and all de reeches' mans in de worl'. Yaas, on Montrahall. Don' you forget. Ahm no peesoup, me!"

There be those living who swear by Heaven, after having been entertained by princes and potentates, they never realized so much unsullied joy at a ball, though led by the queen, as they did at Johnny Beaver's dance, "years ago."

A Cannon Shotted With Gold Coin.

At some period during the French and English war a detachment of the former in bateaux propelled by oar and sail, ran into La Famine, partly for shelter and partly to lose itself from an unrelenting enemy. So closely were they pursued by the English in Durham boats that capture seemed inevitable, and a flag of truce was run up. While negotiations were pending the commander of the French fleet bethought himself of the numerous bags of gold coin stowed away in the flagship, and which would all too soon fall into the possession of the victors unless secreted immediately.

He counseled with his officers with the result that a cannon was unlimbered and the coin poured into its rapacious mouth. After the precious charge had been rammed home the mouth of the cannon was securely plugged and it was then thrown overboard.

In the excitement of the moment no ranges were taken, and nothing but the depth of the water was known for a certainty. Eight fathoms deep, tradition hath it, and somewhere between the Basswood tree and Squaw Island, somewhere between the Gap and Whitefish, and, it might be well said, somewhere between earth and sky, so indefinite were the traditional conjectures.

At any rate the elements interfered in the Frenchman's behalf and after loosing his anchors the Englishman was blown beyond the possibility of victory just as terms had been negotiated. With the first shift of wind the French fleet sailed leading their late adversaries by a full day with a fair wind.

Long years after, a piratical appearing craft cruised the land-locked shores of La Famine for some weeks. Not one of the crew could speak English, but enough of their language was understood to convey the idea with certainty that they were searching for treasure.

Immediately the tradition related above was revived and many speculations were had concerning it. Hank Collins and Jim Lane—old Jim, thought, talked and dreamed of the old smooth bore and its precious charge.

"'Spose they drew the charge before ramming the coin down," queried Lane.

"Probably they did and probably they didn't. They mount as well a fired her after she was loaded, considerin' how scatterin' the article is nowadays," philosophically answered Collins.

Lane had the best head, and he had studied the probabilities and the possibilities attendant upon these incidents, and finally persuaded Collins to go out upon the water and guess at the probable course a storm-driven fleet with no knowledge of the waters they were sailing would naturally take in the search for anchorage and shelter.

"The wind mostly blows sou'west in these parts, and that is most likely the way it was blowin' when the Frenchman was scuddin' for easier weather," reasoned Lane with his partner. "Now observe the range of the Basswood agin the

Pint—swing her off a couple yerks—now keep the Pint clear of the tree about the width of yer hand—steady—and mind that tall tamarack plumb ahead. Now we're dead in the wake of the fleet adrivin'—"

"Which boat had the coin," broke in Collins.

"Dang it, enny on 'em, no matter which. Just supposin' —your tree has slid into the Pint agin—open out and gin yer attention to the ranges. Just supposin' the hull fleet was bowlin' along, wind blowin' a gagger, where now would any sane skipper pint fur? Tell me that Hank Collins."

"Well, if he ware natterally a sailor man he'd hug the shore same's we're adoin', and when the soundin's showed favorable I 'low he'd jam her nose well up toward the long bay aport."

"Eggsakly!" shouted Lane with as much emphasis as though he had found the precise resting place of the French treasure.

The wind was increasing and Lane shipped a pair of mismated oars, and after wetting the thole pins, caught stroke and kept his eyes steadily on the Basswood tree and the "Pint."

The men labored at the oars in silence for some time, and as the wind was with them they did not much mind the increasing waves as they threw the heavy old seine boat right and left. It was not long before the men realized that they were in a gale, and one had to bail a share of the time to keep the boat manageable.

"I say, Hank," suggested Lane, "lets make up into Long Bay and wait for this squali to blow over. Besides, we will see about where the Frenchman dropped his mud-hooks in seventeen hundred and what-was-it?"

"Gad, zounds! Man, but you're long headed! The very

thing—left hand best—the very thing Frenchy must have done—left hand—if he knew much about that kind of sailoring—left hand—which was mostly like Scotch navigation—main strength and ignorance, Jim, main strength and ignorance."

"Say, Mister Collins, it strikes me there is a deal of main strength in this here navigation. See! We're driftin' out of the mouth of the bay and will do some tall pullin' if we don't make leeway that will blow us clean by the Pint to say nothink of getting up into the bay."

Collins made no reply. He pulled at the heavy oars with his eyes shut, and opened them when swinging back for a new hold. The wind had been steadily drawing to westward, thus fairly disputing the right of way with the treasure hunters. The two men saw the point slip past them and realized that it was useless to attempt to get under the lee of the friendly shore not a half mile distant.

Lane was a reasoner and so far had led the "expedition" as he facetiously termed it. Collins was an imitator and not so thoughtful. An idea occurred to him and he called to Lane, pouring the words into his broad back and far too leeward:

"The Frenchman anchored, you say?"

"So I've been told."

"In course—he had to. Let's heave old Ben (a pet name for his anchor) over and see if he'll hold us, and if he does we can take observations, pick up the lost ranges and mebbe fish up the old cannon—'fools for luck,' they say."

"All right," heartily responded Lane, "but first bend on that warping line."

"Show! Ther's fifty feet of line without it, and four fathom's all you'll get here."

"THE OARSMAN WAS HEADLESS"

"Better bend on the other, Hank, you will want lots of hemp to jump at in this sea, let me tell you."

The ropes were united with a "fisherman's bend," and the anchor was poised on the gunwale, flukes pointing upward and downward, and after a second look to see that the rope was all clear, it was dropped over, the boat lifting on being relieved of the weight.

"There," said Collins, paying out the rope, "I calculate thet thar's about the way them runaways did it—bottom fell out?—when they tried to dodge the English—bottom—and lost their——"

Both men stared, each at the other.

The knot just appeared above the water and showed—

"Eight fathom!"

"Henry," said Lane solemnly, "we're within a hundred feet of the cannon! Get ranges, quick, we're dragging old Ben home. It's providence, Hank, nothing short of providence, and I promise now I'm goin' to lead a better life."

"Me, too, Jim. I feel mighty trembly about this spot. Let's give it up. No use anyway, a hundred feet or a hundred mild's all the same to me and you. Come!

"Tell the truth and shame the devil, Hank. I don't feel that the water hereabout is just as solid and sure to float us as it might be. So gin us a hand and we'll get the lines in. But this much I'm willin' to chanst. We'll leave a buoy to mark the ranges and try it a couple of months later in calm weather."

Getting the anchor in, the men headed their boat toward La Famine and as they pulled away before the wind each watched the speck of a buoy, which seemed, like the rainbow, to have a pot of gold at its end. Little was said between them except on landing to exact a promise from each to make no revelations, though all they had to reveal was that an eight-fathom sounding had been made at a spot where they would stake everything they had never found to exceed four. That night two fishermen dreamed of fabulous wealth which, fast as recovered from a rusty old cannon, would fly back to its former resting place.

Early next morning the misty figures of two men could have been dimly seen in a heavy fog approaching each other on a well worn path. They were the treasure hunters of yesterday, and were met by chance. Morning salutations were not in order in this New England descended, cold neighborhood. That formality was a deference strictly reserved for strangers who happened in their midst. Both men looked a little surprised, however, and Collins broke the silence of the wood by asking:

"Wher ye goin'?"

"T' your house. Wher you headin' for?"

"T' see you," frankly answered Collins.

"I dreamed—" They began in one voice.

"Well, tell yours," suggested Lane.

"I dreamed your blamed old cannon," he was getting interested, now, but he did not wish to show too much excitement over a dream. "I dreamed your blamed old cannon lay eight fathom deep in a sink-hole eight fathom across, and on the other side of the hole from our buoy, eight fathom——"

"My dream exactly!" interrupted Lane, who had been paling as Collins progressed.

"We better not wait 'till the summer cams come on, had we Jimmy?"

"No, sir-re! Lets be off now! The fog'll lift before we can get over there, and besides, if it don't none will suspect what we are dragging for," and as Lane finished he cut a small fork from a plum tree and taking the extremities in either hand, the point of union upward, he proposed to take it along as he had located hundreds of wells by dowsing, besides making wonderful use of the same as a divining rod when prospecting for buried treasure at French Creek—a story that may be narrated sometime in "LEGENDARY STORIES OF THE THOUSAND ISLANDS."

The two men stole silently down-shore to their boat, and a moment later were lost in the dense fog of a cold spring's morning. An hour's labor at the oars bringing them near the spot of yesterday's find, they began to penetrate the fog in search of the buoy.

"I caught a glimpse of the Basswood and I dunno but we're too fur to lurard," suggested Lane.

"Lor' amighty! Back her! Backer! A sloop to starboard!" roared Collins. Then Lane took command.

"Pull! Right hand, right—he'll run us down shor' as preachin'! The loonatick's a follerin' us at every move! Steady, now plant your oars ready to pull or push for life the minit he gets nigh to us."

The men sat rigid as statues, their oars pointing straight out from the boat, ready to back water or pull away as the exigencies of the approaching crisis might decree. The fog lifted a little and both men dropped their oars in astonishment as the big, looming sloop suddenly collapsed into the buoy they had put out with their own hands to mark the anchorage.

"What in natur!" began Collins, "was that are phantom some o' your spookery with the water witch of a plum sprout."

"It's a good omen, Henry. I mind some such experience before. Now, say! Not a word of talk after we get within eight fathom of the buoy. Mind, now. So much as a word would spoil all. Why, I helped dig up Captain Kidd's treasure chest on Pig's Foot Island, and stood with one foot on the chest and a lubber said, 'Gimme the spade.' That chest shot out from under me and I dropped down three feet into a hole where it laid. 'Gimme the spade,' said he, and a million in gold coin went into the bowels of the earth with a flash and there ware a smell of brimstone to choke ye. Now we'll take soundin's."

Four fathoms! Five, six—eight! Seven, five, four, and Lane motioned to Collins to fall away. More soundings were rapidly taken, and in a short time the bounds of the pot-hole were fairly located. They discovered that it dropped off precipitously four fathoms, was eight fathoms wide, as many in depth, and the lead showed hard bottom. They then set about a systematic dragging of anchor and grapnel in the hope, if possible, of getting foul of the French gun and bringing it, charge and all, to the surface. Time and again they rowed over the charmed spot only to find their labor vain.

Collins pointed significantly to the plum sprout. Lane nervously grasped it by the ends, held it out from his body, palms upward, and gripped the branches which converged in an ugly knot at a level with his eyes. Perspiration fell from his face as the witch pointed astern.

Collins backed water.

Down, down turned the plum sprout, wringing the bark as the boat moved slowly over the "hole." Then it turned upward as they passed beyond its rim. The experiment was tried by approaching the point of strongest attraction from different directions until it was well located. Then the anchor and grapnel were again brought into service and the course dragged over and again.

Collins' line brought up solid and he opened his lips to speak, but a warning look from Lane reminded him of the consequence. Just then Lane's line fouled on something equally solid. The lines were strained taut and the boat brought to a position directly over the object. Again the plum sprout was tried, and they were not surprised when it turned straight downward and stopped at a perpendicular.

Collins drew breath as if about to speak, but Lane was watching him and cut off the words fatal to success before they were uttered.

The treasure-seekers were by this time nearly beside themselves with excitement in which fear played not a small part. They hove the side of the boat down until the water almost came in, and then by stepping over to the opposite side rocked it, the while taking in the slack of the ropes as they gave to the strain. After repeated efforts the object upon which the anchors had fouled yielded, and was brought slowly and laboriously to the surface, its advance heralded by bubbles of gas.

Covered with rust, mud and black ooze the Frenchman's gun lay at the surface. The prize was at their fingers' ends. Tremblingly they pulled on the ropes which had fallen into notches already worn in the wale. So interested were they that they did not hear the approach of another boatman.

Clank, clank!

The clatter and squeak of a pair of heavy oars caught their attention, and they faced about as one man.

A large boat, propelled by oars, was approaching, the single occupant pulling a long, steady stroke in time with the long, lazy swells that seemed at each rise ready to give up the effort to go farther. Yet they ceased not, but ran ahead of the long sweep of the oars as if teasing the occupant to race.

Clank, clank!

Shade of Charon! The blood of the fishermen stood still, and their amazement was unbounded.

The oarsman was headless!

Straight toward the treasure he pointed his boat, sightless as he was, and his severed neck showing a ghastly wound as he bent to his oars. Steadily he forged ahead so close now that the ripple around the stem came to their ears. The boat was battered and scarred, built upon strange lines, and a hole had been broken into her bow as though she had been raked by a six-pounder. Long weeds trailed in her wake which appeared as a stream of fire, and mosses flourished on her runboards.

All this and more the treasure-seekers saw in less time than is required to relate it. Nearer and plainer, now, sounded the chilling——

Clank, clank!

And the men were aroused by the instinct of self-preservation. Each seized an oar in one hand, with the other holding to the rope by which the cannon was suspended. They were now thoroughly alarmed at this uncanny visitor who occasionally turned to right and left in his seat as if looking over his headless shoulders to take his bearings, or perhaps more properly, dead reckonings.

"Now!" shouted Lane.

"Strike!" echoed Collins.

Fatal words! The charm was broken, for no sooner had the men spoken as with one voice than——

Boom! Ba-r-r-gn!

The cannon was fired at the first vocal sound and burst into a thousand fragments while its precious charge was scattered over the waste of waters toward the rising sun. Both men dropped in the boat and for a minute neither could speak.

When they had sufficiently recovered their senses to rise, the apparation had gone apparently as swiftly as the treasure which they had just as good as secured. The ropes burned off the moment the discharge occurred and down went the anchors if indeed they were not blown to atoms.

Silently, ruefully, sadly the fishermen shipped their oars and pulled away for home as stoutly as their shattered nerves and disappointed hopes would permit. Each desired to put the blame of failure upon the other, and an argument as to who spoke first and thus dispelled the charm, ended in a solemn agreement never to reveal a word. But each told his wife, "she" told her sister, and so the community was soon reveling in the doubtful story. Year after year the exact spot is shown the summer guest, and to the incredulous proof is forthcoming when with lead and line the outlines of the rim to the pot-hole are located by taking soundings, and then there is the Basswood tree, the Point and the Bay to confirm the rest of the story.

The Legend of Calumet Island.

There is abundance of evidence which goes to prove that had the scene of events in Longfellow's immortal Hiawatha been located at the Thousand Islands, the Manatoana, or " Garden of the Great Spirit," of the Iroquois and Algonquins, the poem would have been true to the legendary origin of Hiawatha. Read with that idea in mind, one will be surprised at the many striking passages which apply to the St. Lawrence with more force than to the Lake Superior region in which the poet has depicted the principal events of the legend.

In 1843, Ossahinta and Dehatkatons, two Onondaga chiefs related the legend of the god of fishing and rivers to Mr. Clark who carefully wrote out the story and filed it in the archives of the New York Historical Society. He thus translates the narration of the two chiefs :

Hundreds of years ago, Ta-oun-ya-wat-ha, the Deity who presides over fisheries and streams, came down from his dwelling place in the clouds to visit the inhabitants of the earth. He had been deputed by the Great and Good Spirit, Ha-wane-u, to visit the streams and clear the channels from all obstructions, to seek out the good things of the country through which he intended to pass, that they might be more generally disseminated among all the good people of the earth—especially to point out to them the most excellent fishing grounds, and to bestow upon them other acceptable gifts. About this time, two young men of the Onondaga Nation were listlessly gazing over the calm blue waters of the Lake of a Thousand Isles. During their reverie they espied, as they thought, far in the distance, a single white speck, beautifully dancing over the bright blue waters, and while they watched the object with the most intense anxiety, it seemed to increase in magnitude, and moved as if approaching the place where they were concealed, most anxiously awaiting the event of the visitation of so singular an object—for at this time no canoes had ever made their appearance in the direction from whence this was approaching. As the object neared the shore, it proved in semblance to be a venerable looking man, calmly seated in a canoe of pure white, very curiously constructed, and much more ingeniously wrought than those in use among the tribes of the country. Like a cygnet upon the wide blue sea, so sat the canoe of To-oun-ya-wat-ha, upon the Lake of a Thousand Isles.

As a frail branch drifts towards the rushing cataract, so coursed the white canoe over the rippling waters, propelled by the strong arm of the god of the river. Deep thought sat on the brow of the gray headed mariner; penetration marked his eye, and deep dark mystery pervaded his countenance. With a single oar he silently paddled his light trimmed bark along the shore, as if seeking a commodious haven of rest. He soon turned the prow of his fragile vessel into the estuary of the "double river," and made fast to the western shore. He majestically ascended the steep bank, nor stopped till he had gained the loftiest summit of the western hill. Then silently gazing around as if to examine the country, he became enchanted with the view, and drawing his stately form to its utmost height, he exclaimed in accents of the wildest enthusiasm, Osh-wah-kee, Osh-wah-kee.

He approached the two young hunters, recounts Dr. Hough, gained their confidence, and having drawn from them a knowledge of the difficulties under which they labored, disclosed to them the spirituality of his character, and the object of his mission. He invited them to attend him in his passage up the river, and they witnessed many things which could only be accounted for as miracles, or be described but in the wonders of Indian mythology. He ascended to the lesser lakes, placed all things in proper order for the comfort and sustenance of man, taught them how to cultivate corn and beans, which had not before been grown by them, made the fishing ground free, and opened to all the uninterrupted pursuit of game. He distributed among mankind the fruits of the earth, and removed all obstructions from the navigable streams. Being pleased with his success, he assumed the character and habits of a man, and received the name Hi-a-wat-ha, (signifying " very wise man,") and fixed his residence on the beautiful shores of Cross Lake. After a time, the country became alarmed by a hostile invasion, when he called a council of all the tribes from the east and the west, and in a long harangue urged upon them the importance of uniting themselves in a league for their common defense and mutual happiness. They deliberated upon his advice, and the next day adopted and ratified the league of union which he recommended. Hi-a-wat-ha, having brought this council to a close, and as the assembled tribes were about to separate, on their return home, arose in a dignified manner, and thus addressed them:

" Friends and Brothers :—I have now fulfilled my mission upon earth ; I have done everything which can be done at present for the good of this great people. Age, infirmity and distress, sit heavily upon me. During my sojourn among you I have removed all obstructions from your streams. Canoes can now pass everywhere. I have given you good fishing waters and good hunting grounds. I have taught you how to cultivate corn and beans, and have learned you the art of making cabins. Many blessings I have liberally bestowed upon you.

Lastly, I have now assisted you to form an everlasting league and covenant of strength and friendship, for your future safety and protection. If you preserve it without the admission of other people, you will always be free, numerous and mighty. If other nations are admitted to your councils, they will sow jealousies among you, and you will become enslaved, few and feeble. Remember these words: they are the last you will hear from the lips of Hi-a-wat-ha. Listen, my friends, the Great-Master-of-Breath calls me to go. I have patiently waited his summons. I am ready: Farewell."

As the wise man closed his speech, there burst upon the ears of the assembled multitude, the cheerful sounds of the most delightful singing voices. The whole sky seemed filled with the sweetest melody of celestial music; and Heaven's high arch echoed and re-echoed the touching strains, till the whole vast assembly was completely absorbed in rapturous ecstasy. Amidst the general confusion which now prevailed, and while all eyes were turned towards the etherial regions, Hi-a-wat-ha was seen majestically seated in his canoe, gracefully rising higher and higher above their heads through the air, until he became entirely lost from the view of the assembled throng, who witnessed his wonderful ascent in mute and admiring astonishment—while the fascinating music gradually became more plaintive and low, and finally sweetly expired in the softest tones upon their ears, as the wise man Hi-a-wat-ha, the god-like Ta-oun-ya-wat-ha, retired from their sight, as mysteriously as he first appeared from The Lake of a Thousand Isles, and, concludes Dr. Hough, quietly entered the regions inhabited only by the favorites of the great and good spirit Ha-wah-ne-u.

That the reader may the better understand the legend of which these pages treat, a portion of Longfellow's "Song of Hiawatha" is here reproduced:

THE PEACE PIPE.

On the Mountains of the Prairie,
On the great Red Pipe-stone Quarry,
Gitche Manito, the mighty,
He the Master of Life, descending,
On the red crags of the quarry,
Stood erect, and called the nations,
Called the tribes of men together.
  From his footprints* flowed a river,†
Leaped into the light of morning,
O'er the precipice plunging downward
Gleamed like Ishkoodah, the comet.
And the spirit, stooping earthward,
With his finger on the meadow
Traced a winding pathway for it,
Saying to it, "Run in this way!"
  From the red stone of the quarry
With his hand he broke a fragment,
Moulded it into a pipe-head,
Shaped and fashioned it with figures;
From the margin of the river
Took a long reed for a pipe-stem,

* The Great Lakes. † The St. Lawrence.

A LEGEND OF CALUMET ISLAND.

With its dark green leaves upon it;
Filled the pipe with bark of willow,
With the bark of the red willow;
Breathed upon the neighboring forest,
Made its great boughs chafe together,
Till in flame they burst and kindled;
And erect upon the mountains,
Gitche Manito, the mighty,
Smoked the CALUMET, THE PEACE-PIPE,
As a signal to the nations.

And the smoke rose slowly, slowly,
Through the tranquil air of morning,
First a single line of darkness,
Then a denser, bluer vapor,
Then a snow-white cloud unfolding,
Like the tree-tops of the forest,
Ever rising, rising, rising,
Till it touched the top of heaven,
Till it broke against the heaven,
And rolled outward all around it.

From the Vale of Tawasentha,
From the Valley of Wyoming,
From the Groves of Tuscaloosa,
From the far-off Rocky Mountains,
From the Northern lakes and rivers
All the tribes beheld the signal,
Saw the distant smoke ascending,
The Pukwana of the Peace-Pipe.

And the Prophets of the nations
Said: " Behold it, the Pukwana!
By this signal from afar off,
Bending like a wand of willow,

Waving like a hand that beckons,
Gitche Manito, the mighty,
Calls the tribes of men together,
Calls the warriors to his council!"
　Down the rivers, o'er the prairies,
Came the warriors of the nations,
Came the Delawares and Mohawks,
Came the Choctaws and Camanches,
Came the Shoshones and Blackfeet,
Came the Pawnees and Omahas,
Came the Mandans and Dacotahs,
Came the Hurons and Ojibways.
All the warriors drawn together
By the signal of the Peace-Pipe,
To the Mountains of the Prairie,
To the great Red Pipe-stone Quarry.
　And they stood there on the meadow,
With their weapons and their war-gear,
Painted like the leaves of Autumn,
Painted like the sky of morning,
Wildly glaring at each other ;
In their faces stern defiance,
In their hearts the feuds of ages,
The hereditary hatred,
The ancestral thirst of vengeance.
　Gitche Manito, the mighty,
The creator of the nations,
Looked upon them with compassion,
With paternal love and pity ;
Looked upon their wrath and wrangling
But as quarrels among children,
But as feuds and fights of children!

Over them he stretched his right hand,
To subdue their stubborn natures,
To allay their thirst and fever,
By the shadow of his right hand ;
Spake to them with voice majestic
As the sound of far-off waters,
Falling into deep abysses,
Warning, chiding, spake in this wise : —
 "O my children! my poor children!
Listen to the words of wisdom,
Listen to the words of warning,
From the lips of the Great Spirit,
From the Master of Life, who made you :
 "I have given you lands to hunt in,
I have given you streams to fish in,
I have given you bear and bison,
I have given you roe and reindeer,
I have given you brant and beaver,
Filled the marshes full of wild-fowl,
Filled the rivers full of fishes ;
Why then are you not contented?
Why then will you hunt each other?
 "I am weary of your quarrels,
Weary of your wars and bloodshed,
Weary of your prayers for vengeance,
Of your wranglings and dissensions ;
All your strength is in your union,
All your danger is in discord ;
Therefore be at peace henceforward,
And as brothers live together.
 "I will send a prophet to you,
A Deliverer of the nations,

Who shall guide you and shall teach you,
Who shall toil and suffer with you.
If you listen to his counsels,
You will multiply and prosper;
If his warnings pass unheeded,
You will fade away and perish!
   " Bathe now in the stream before you,
Wash the war-paint from your faces,
Wash the blood-stains from your fingers,
Bury your war-clubs and your weapons,
Break the red stone from this quarry,
Mould and make it into Peace-Pipes,
Take the reeds that grow beside you,
Deck them with your brightest feathers,
Smoke the calumet together,
And as brothers live henceforward!"
   Then upon the ground the warriors
Threw their cloaks and shirts of deerskin,
Threw their weapons and their war-gear,
Leaped into the rushing river,
Washed the war-paint from their faces.
Clear above them flowed the water,
Clear and limpid from the footprints
Of the Master of Life descending;
Dark below them flowed the water,
Soiled and stained with streaks of crimson,
As if blood were mingled with it!
   From the river came the warriors,
Clean and washed from all their war-paint;
On the banks their clubs they buried,
Buried all their warlike weapons.
Gitche Manito, the mighty,

The Great Spirit, the creator,
Smiled upon his helpless children !
And in silence all the warriors
Broke the red stone of the quarry,
Smoothed and formed it into Peace-Pipes.
Broke the long reeds by the river,
Decked them with their brightest feathers,
And departed each one homeward.
While the Master of Life, ascending.
Through the opening of cloud-curtains,
Through the doorways of the heaven,
Vanished from before their faces,
In the smoke that rolled around him,
The Pukwana of the Peace-Pipe.

The Indian name for French creek, in the village of Clayton, was Weteringhra-Guentere, the "Fallen Fort," or perhaps more literally, "the place where the hills fell down." An ancient and rude fortification at the mouth of French Creek was the traditional boundary line between the Iroquois and Algonquin nations whom the first white navigator of the St. Lawrence found engaged in a war which began before time was fixed even by uncertain tradition.

The war was said to have originated with a hunting party composed of a half dozen young men of each nation. One party followed an elk many leagues and returned without game whatsoever. The other party then set out and meeting with immediate success the lately vanquished party was compelled to do squaw work—skinning, dressing and cooking. The jealousy of the latter was now aggravated by humiliation, and a feud was engendered which their few living descendants secretly cherish to this day.

This feud was precipitated long after the advent of Hiawatha, the river god, and in violation of his admonitions. After this murderous war had been carried on many years the land was taken from the Mississaguas by the Great Spirit who was more than ever displeased with his chosen whom he had placed in the Manatoana, this Garden of Eden, only to have the compact of peace rudely violated.

An island in the St. Lawrence, opposite Clayton, presents in the contour of its shores, and general topography, a wonderful resemblance to an Indian pipe, and for this reason long ago it was called CALUMET. This island it is claimed is no other than the Calumet, the gigantic Peace-Pipe, smoked by Gitche Manito, the mighty, "as a signal to the nations," the ascending smoke from which attracted the attention of the Prophets of the nations upon whose interpretation the tribes of men were immediately called together at Manatoana, the Garden of the Great Spirit, the Mille Iles of the French voyageurs, the Thousand Islands of today.

Gitche Manito sent messengers to bear away the country of the Mississaguas and they came with a great skin blanket which was let down by the four corners. Into this blanket Manatoana, the Garden of the Great Spirit, with its rivers, lakes and mountains, was carefully placed, the great Calumet in the center. The blanket with its burden was borne away skyward, but as the wondering Mississaguas gazed upward they were terrified at discovering that the messengers had broken their hold. The garden and the great blanket came tumbling down and was broken into a thousand fragments— and thus originated the Thousand Islands. The Calumet was fairly pulverized, a token that the covenant between the Great Spirit and the nations was no more. The Mississaguas were no longer the chosen people. They had broken the pledge to keep peace among themselves and Gitche Manito had made his anger manifest by the significant breaking of the Calumet, the pipe of peace.

Hence, Weteringhra-Guentere, "the place where the hills fell down."

Daniel Millikin, American.

Your grandfather and I settled in this neighborhood in 1806, making the long journey from Connecticut with one horse and a pair of oxen, camping by the way wherever night overtook us. We were married but a few days before setting out, and you may be sure it was not a luxurious wedding journey, but stout hearts and bright hopes kept us good company.

Our new home overlooked Lake Ontario, which seemed to me broad as the ocean, for no trace of the farther shore could be seen. Full five years we worked from daylight to dark, and then had really less than we brought with us. Your father, no, grandfather, was a tanner and currier and had often talked of returning to his trade, but he could not readily get such employment even in this new country. One day he came from La Famine, and turning the horse loose at the door, came in and sat by the fireplace in silence a long time. My heart sank when he did speak. We were to leave our home and my parents, who had followed us, and go to Canada, where he had contracted to work as foreman in a tannery, and was to receive eight dollars in gold every week for his services. It was a bold stroke which to our minds foretold great wealth, and yet we were reluctant to leave our little clearing and go among a strange people in a foreign land. Besides, the thought of living within the king's domains was not pleasant.

Rumors of trouble between the young republic and Great Britain had reached us from time to time, but the single newspaper that came fortnightly said England dare not fight again, besides should there be war, Canada would side with us and it, too, become free. At length our fears were put aside and we left by sail, there were no steamers then, and two days later landed far up the Canadian shore at a little village containing a church, a few log houses and the tannery store.

For a while we saved money, but with the ugly war news the times grew harder and harder until we were compelled to take store pay entirely. When war was actually declared your grandfather, and the four Americans he had brought with him, decided to return home since in the heat of argument they had already gotten into trouble with the tannery hands. They were good workmen and had obtained such favor with the contractors that, to induce them to stay, the pay in gold was resumed and they were assured that should they remain they would be exempt from military duty. Then came the report that the British had burned Boston. That decided our people that they must go back and defend their homes, but they tarried a few days in the hope that it was a false report made to encourage loyalty in the Canadas.

One morning we heard the booming of cannon at York, now Toronto, and our men made no effort to conceal their joy at General Pike's bold attack and subsequent capture of the city. All Canada was in high dudgeon, and our little colony suffered its share of abuse, and we were given to understand that we must repress our feelings or suffer the consequences. Although the season was advancing and lake navigation dangerous, the Americans began at once the secret construction of a large bateau in which we were all to return. Every man in the village was ordered to arm and report at the church whence they were to march to the recapture of York. You may be sure haste was made in the construction of the boat, the builders paying no heed to the warning to equip for war. It was completed two days after the militia had departed, and our hopes ran high while loading it with stores for the return to home, friends and country.

While thus engaged six mounted redcoats appeared upon the rise above us and demanded a surrender. Our men were armed and had agreed to fight if the officers came to press them into the service, but your grandfather was the only one to stand his ground and fire. His shot was returned with a volley, and he fell with a bullet in his arm. Springing to his feet he began to reload, and as the soldiers were preparing to fire another volley I ran in front of him and dared them to shoot a woman. Blood trickled from his hand, and as I tried to bandage his wound the brutal soldiers closed about us and your grandfather was bound to a saddle before I could dress his arm which hung limp at his side. They started away and I attempted to follow, but the soldiers threatened to shoot me also if I made further ado. My husband bade me return to the house and mind the children, and as they galloped away I saw a pistol held to his head for shouting to me that he would be back that very night.

I watched them out of sight, and then with a breaking heart entered the cabin. There I found Ruth Sophronia and Thankful Amanda armed with table knives in emulation of the spirit of America, while little Asa Ebenezer was pouring powder from the horn into his milk.

The vision of their poor wounded father, borne away to an unknown fate was before me day and night, and I nearly worried myself into insanity. Week after week wore away and yet no word came to relieve my distress or confirm my fears. Frequent stories of butcheries by Indians employed in the British service kept me in constant alarm lest such a fate overtake me and my helpless children. Often I took them into the woods when Indians were in the neighborhood, and came back only when compelled by cold and hunger. There were few neighbors left, and those I dare not trust for there were among them those whom I believed had informed the officers of our intended departure. As the winter came on a sense of my utter loneliness bore me down, and to return to my parents became the whole subject of my thought. It would soon be a physical necessity since the provisions were low and the money reduced to a single gold coin. In the fear of being massacred the few people in the village were preparing to leave, and at this I was determined to face any danger than remain entirely alone.

To recross the lake at this season was next to impossible, even for experienced sailors. I knew the St. Lawrence river must be frozen over at Kingston which was strongly garrisoned by the British. A wounded soldier brought me word that your grandfather had been taken to that post for trial, and that settled a purpose to return that way in the hope of seeing my husband, if but for a moment. A farmer was engaged to carry us to Kingston, and after nearly a week's travel in deep snow we reached the barracks. The farmer made inquiry for my husband and was told that he had been taken to Montreal and shot for treason.

I did not faint—women did not have the habit then—neither was I greatly surprised, for I had already learned something of the severity of martial law. There was no time to shed bitter tears over our utterly forlorn condition, and to make the situation completely dismal, the river at this point, where I had hoped to cross, was a sea of floating ice. Home seemed as far away as at the outset.

We were kindly cared for at a log tavern by the landlady, herself American born, until the first fair day, when I resolutely set out with my three children to find a crossing farther down the River. It was said there was firm ice from shore to shore at Brockville, fifty miles distant, but the task did not appall me for the hope of getting my children to their grandparents gave me courage. Bravely, then, we traveled a country filled with hostile Indians and soldiers, to my mind one fully as wicked as the other, remaining over night with the settlers except once when the distance between neighbors was too far to be covered in a day. We passed that night by the remains of a fire not three hours deserted, and ate a little dried venison which a farmer's wife had put in the hand of one of the children as we left. One morning a great hullabaloo was raised about the house of some kind people who cared for us by making a bed on the floor in front of the fireplace. A loud rap at the door, then a gruff voice shouted:

" Open and surrender or we will fire the house!"

In alarm the door was thrown open and twenty dragoons were discovered about the little hut. An officer looked about the house sharply and said information had reached him that a female spy was harbored within and must go with him to the barracks, as well as the farmer whose loyalty he said they now had reason to suspect. I presented myself and children and told the story of my travels. Our pitiful condition must

"SIX MOUNTED REDCOATS APPEARED."

have shamed him, for after consulting with another officer and asking me a great many questions, he threw a silver piece into the door and they rode away.

The dear Lord only knows what we suffered the next day, facing a stinging norther which came up after the rain of the night before. On, on, I went, carrying first one child and then the other, and sometimes two. An occasional glimpse of the American shore had kept up my courage all along the weary miles, but fields of moving ice prevented my crossing. Home almost in sight, yet far, far away, and I was so weary. The trial was telling upon the children too, and I prayed that they might be given strength from above until we crossed the lines and came among my own countrymen.

I cut the village of Brockville short, fearing another ordeal of being mistaken for a spy. Another hour's travel brought us to a point where the ice seemed firm all the way across to Morristown, where were stationed American troops.

As we struck out on the ice the children were knee deep in the water, and about us were whirlpools caused by the water drawing down through airholes in the ice. I shuddered at these dark vortexes, in size sufficient to swallow us at a gulp, and it was only by winding and turning that we avoided these new dangers. Would either of my three babes survive such unnatural exposure? Would the frail bridge support us? We would face still greater dangers rather than turn back. The water froze to our skirts, the weary little feet dragged heavily at my side, and I felt the hold on my dress weakening as the frost-bitten fingers became numb, and— heavens, was my baby boy freezing in my arms. I strove blindly on willing to die if I could but get my perishing children to friends.

A loud shout startled my heart into feverish action at the

thought of help, only to all but stop at the fear of another encounter with the redcoats. But the Lord is good. I recognized the uniform of the American militia, and the next moment strong arms bore us all across the treacherous channel to firmer ice where the dragoons were waiting to make a speedy flight with us to the barracks at Morristown. The children, scarcely able to speak, were rolled in blankets by the surgeon's wife who dared not bring them to the fire, and in a few days recovered their wonted activity. When my story was told I heard many threats among the rough troopers, one actually proposing to cross and burn Brockville that very night.

After remaining a few days we were sufficiently recovered to resume our journey, but we did no more walking. Our new friends provided a way for us nearly half the distance, and the remainder we covered by short rides with neighbors. It was with a heavy heart that I approached the scene of our first housekeeping, besides the time had now come when my children must learn the truth of their father's absence. My parents were overjoyed at our return and received us as from the dead. I bought eight yards of black calico and made it into a dress for Sundays. The winter passed slowly enough and when the birds came with spring I was more than ever disheartened as each note seemed to recall the happy plans we had made for converting our forest home into a blooming field.

One Sunday I had a call from Neighbor Rasbach, whose poor, weak wife had died of the fever——

"Well, you needn't 'a thought I was dead," broke in grandfather a little snappishly, and to our surprise he told the remainder of the story himself in these words:

When the dragoons captured me I was in great pain from my wound, but the officers made no offer to bandage my arm, not even after reaching York. In the garrison the only attention I had was to be chained to a post like a slave, and have a cold meal brought once a day. For a week this neglect continued, and then twenty of us were fastened in the hold of a schooner and taken to Kingston.

After a few days' miserable treatment there we were started for Montreal in bateaux, the officer compelling me to labor at the oars although all but dead with pain from my wounds. At the rapids so closely did we pass to the islands that at times the branches of trees brushed the boat as we passed, but escape was impossible in my disabled condition, although I was sorely tempted to jump over and swim, trusting that their slow flint-locks would give me time to reach the shore. At Montreal we were penned in a guard house and not only suffered neglect but were tortured with false reports of British success. A formal charge of treason was read to me,and what I suppose was the death penalty was delivered in French. I was still in total darkness as to my fate.

One afternoon the American prisoners were roughly ordered out of the log prison, and under a strong guard marched out of the garrison as we verily believed to our death. For two days we were marched westward in ignorance of our destination, or the purpose in removing us. Then from a hill we saw a flag of truce and soldiers in the American uniform. There we were told they had brought us out to fight our countrymen, but before we were armed our enemies surrendered and we were free.

After the first excitement was over I determined to go to my family, if indeed they had not met the fate of a hundred deaths which I fancied they had met at the hands of the Indians, or from starvation, exposure or wolves. Back we marched as rapidly as possible to Fort Ticonderoga, whence I, not being in the regular service, was permitted to depart.

I chose the Canadian thoroughfare and traveled mostly at night fearing to meet the British soldiery. I crossed the St. Lawrence to Morristown for the purpose of going to my old home and crossing the lake in search of wife and children. At the barracks the account of my capture recalled the rescue of the mother and children from their perilous trip across the ice, and I knew from that moment they were safe. I came away at once and a week later found your grandmother in widow's weeds planting some hollyhocks in the yard.

"Let me help you, mother," I said. She just turned around, fell into my arms, and—had a good cry. Her parents gave me a wonderful welcome and got up a great dinner in honor of my return, but somehow no one had much of an appetite.

The companions who fled at my capture joined General Pike's forces and with them retreated when York was retaken, and afterward engaged in the battle at Sackets Harbor, and, Eben, if ever I hear you say another word about joining Canada to the states, you will not get the bay colt. Remember!

Wind and Weather Permitting.

The La Famine fishermen arranged a boat race that is well remembered by the older settlers, leastwise those who saw it with the feverish imagination of youth. Far and wide the event was heralded on quarter-sheet posters in this style:

GRAND REGATTA.

A Grand Sailing Regatta will be holden at La Famine, wind and weather permitting, on
FRIDAY, JULY, 4TH, 18—
Open to all American fishing boats under 24 feet keel.
(The "Sophia" barred.)
Owned on this end of the Lake.
Purse, $50.00, &c.

Spring fishing, attended by good luck, was over, so those

now resting from their labors made general preparations for the race. July Fourth there were 22 entries of fishing craft, many of them fitted with suspiciously new sails, others with a "cloth" recently added to the leech, and at least two with ill-fitting borrowed sails of larger dimensions than the ordinary business rig. Off the shore came a smart breeze which had freshened not a little when the contestants anchored in line across a narrow reach from the lake, jibs furled, booms aswing, mainsail filling and backing at the caprice of the wind, and picked crews all alert. On the shore a crowd is waiting for a signal for the start, the while somewhat jealously discussing the rig of a yacht with flying jib and a string of flags, manned by a crew of boys in duck pants, and steered with a wheel.

Bang! A pistol shot from the hands of the referee, a justice of the peace so everlastingly dignified as to compel his own boys and girls to call him "'Squire."

Bang! Twenty-two jibs shoot up the forestay, twenty-two cables are slipped, twenty-two tillers hard up, twenty-two prows fall away, and twenty-two fishing boats, clean as a cabined steam yacht, cleave the blue waters and churn up a wave of foam in a grand charge for the lee shore not thirty rods distant.

Hard alee!

The sailing master of the boat having the favored position comes into the wind and then with his starboard tacks aboard claims the right of way, compelling the first comer to go in stays so quickly that the gravel bags fall overboard, others to ware and some to gybe. He takes the bowsprit from one too venturesome, and runs his horn through the leech of another who had gone about in the vain hope of laying to windward of the fleet. Another boat with broken rudder is run out high and dry on the beach; another is turned completely over, the crew perching along the keel unheeded by the more fortunate "defenders."

While the boats are dodging each other in a confusion of flapping sails, loud orders, and cheers from the shore, a big fellow is setting a gaff-topsail, "just fer to put on style," as Bone Marceau expressed it. But pride goeth before a fall, Mr. Big One, and ere the extra sail is fairly set the halyards foul and the sail flaps away with tack adrift and clewline spinning out until it reaches a kink, when the topsail suddenly fills, bellies away to leeward, and the boat within an inch of capsizing, ships so much water as to make her all but unmanageable, and she is withdrawn from the race. Seventeen boats overstrained with a crowd of canvas thrash the narrow waters into a choppy sea. The Bluebird breaks her mast off close to the jaws, and is towed into a friendly cove.

Interest in the contest narrows down to the three or four in the lead. Nancy Marceau has already observed in the confusion of sails what others have not. She has seen the Fancy, with the F changed by some miscreant with a little coal tar into an apology for an N, stand straight through the reach without once tacking.

"Is Job sailing the Nancy-er-Fancy?" asked young Lane, looking at Nancy as though she ought to know.

"Dunno," she curtly replied with flushing cheek and a look that gave the lie to the words. "It's none of my business and less of yours, Jim Lane."

"That might be and then agin it mightn't," and Jim made a telescope of his hands to cut off the subject.

Out of the reach into the broad bay sped the boats urged by a stiffening breeze, their windward runboards lined with bags of gravel which quickly shifted for the other tack, keeps them right side up and in sailing trim. The Fancy rounds the outer mark followed by the Saucy Jane and Crazy Jack close upon her. No sooner is each boat fairly around the buoy and before the wind on the return than a big lugsail is run up the mast, a boom shot out and as the sails fill the boats fairly fly over the course, each carrying a bone in her teeth which is plainly discerned by the participants, in spirit, at least, on the shore.

"Job is ragging it to her for first prize, sure," remarked a young neighbor lad who had made one trip on the upper lakes and returned with a lot of knowledge, and a blue flannel shirt ornamented with crossed anchors in white braid.

"He can't steer a raft across the canawl and fetch the furder side," sneeringly remarked old Marceau.

"He'll rag the stick outen her if he don't take in his washing afore ten minutes," he continued, and even as he spoke the spectators discovered the whitecaps chasing each other in the wake of the flying racers. The Crazy Jack was farthest astern and caught the squall almost unawares. She lifted and plunged, then an ominous cracking forward proved trouble from an unlooked-for source. The forefoot twisted out of the step and the mast already bending forward, pitched into the boiling waters under her bows, tearing out the deck and snapping backstays like threads. The hardy crew, wet to the skin, very quickly cleared up the wreck and with the jibboom lashed to the splintered deck and a bit of sail bagging from it, they scudded past the inner buoy, and by dint of vigorous bailing succeeded in making a landing without further damage. Of the fleet which started in the race one after another had dropped out until only the Fancy and the Saucy Jane remained. After the disaster to the Crazy Jack, which was highly appreciated by the crowd on shore, the two remaining approached the inner buoy which they were to turn and then again cover the course. The Fancy came on and just when abreast the mark furled her lug sail and as the sheet was hauled in by a run forward she swung around to the wind and heeled over until her keel showed clear of the waves, and she seemed drifting to windward from the momentum accrued in circling the mark.

Crack!

The onlookers are treated to another long-hoped-for bit of excitement. The Fancy's topmast had broken off at the truck and her peak was dangling in the lifts. A figure is going aloft, hand over hand, on the windward stays. The wind strengthens and the figure shrinks closer to the stump of the mast.

"Hard luck; I'm sorry," said Jim Lane, and he caught Nancy Marceau watching the figure with an intensity that almost betrayed her recognition of the nimble sailor.

"Jim, do you think he will fall?" spoke Nancy boldly and yet almost tearfully.

"It's none o' my business, much less yourn," mockingly replied the ungallant Jim, smiling at his own cleverness.

Old Marceau watched the repairs with a sailor's admiration for a display of skill in close quarters, but his shaded eyes failed to recognize young Collins else he would not have complimented the good seamanship which quickly resulted in securing a block to the stump of the mast, and after reeving a halyard into it the peak was set up, a single reef having been put in the mainsail and jib in the meantime. Then the Fancy, far in the rear, began the battle afresh amid the cheers of the sailors and fishermen who had gathered down the shore the better to see the contest for the supremacy of the fishing fleet.

"Now," said Joby as he resumed a position on the quarter and steadied the tiller by the round turn of a rope belayed to windward. "we shall overhaul the Saucy if that stick holds."

"Yes," said the man tending jib sheet, "she is carrying too much sail now. See her heel down and luff. I tell you these seas deaden the headway and throw her too much to leeward when her luff is slapping like that."

Tacking to the outer mark was not making rapid headway, and the gain counted upon for the Fancy's getting down to steady work was not so much as her galiant crew had hoped. A plank was run out to windward and a man, Johnny Beaver, clambered out toward the end as the boat careened, and quickly slid down again as she straightened up. It was truly a comical sight, this man dangling in mid-air at an elevation of nearly forty-five degrees as the boat yielded to a puff and lay down. Successively rising and falling he more than once took a ducking from a big comber that reached up and hit him all over when he was a trifle slow about sliding back, laughingly remarking: "Never tooch me."

The Saucy Jane a mile to windward was nearing the mark, every joint squeaking with the strain of canvas. She was shipping water like a canal boat crossing the lake when——

Zip!

The clewline tackle stranded, then broke, and her sail slid down the boom almost to the mast. The next instant she bore away before the wind and was running like a wildcat away from the coveted mark with her helpless crew, the helm hard down and the rudder square across her stern, plowing up the water like an exposed propeller blade. Only the most skillful seamanship such as is developed in the fishing craft of the Great Lakes, prevented a disaster before she could be brought to the wind and her sails reefed. This last accident brought the boats very close together and as they stood out for the mark all eyes were centered upon the scene and many were the speculations as to the outcome.

"There she goes," a dozen voices shouted as one boat, not half the crowd knew which, rounded the mark and squared away for the home buoy. The next instant the other maneuvered in the same manner and the two boats threaten to capsize, first on one side and then on the other, so heavy is the roll. A bright, new lugsail is sent up, and a cheer goes up as the home boat is recognized in the rear but now fast overhauling her competitor with the crew in white duck. The Fancy, startled at the strain of another sail, leaped forward like a deer, and the rolling subsiding in a measure by the balancing of the new sail, she steadied down for the six-mile run with less foam and froth in a very business-like way.

"A starn chase is a long chase," commented old Marceau, as he recognized the advantage to the boat of the son of his dead enemy.

"Why don't them dandy marines stick out a lugger, the lubbers," he continued.

A voice cried "Shame," but it was drowned in the loud huzzas as the Fancy passed the other, one of the crew holding out a rope as if offering a tow.

The already vanquished foreigner ran up his lugsail, peak down, not daring to set the whole sail, but he was yet slow and the Fancy had already near a minute the lead. In a few minutes the contest was over and a hundred hands met the Fancy and lifted her clear of the water high and dry on the beach the moment she reached the shore. The stranger picked up his anchor, dipped his ensign, fired a brass gun and acknowledged defeat in a very naval-like manner which quickly created a feeling of admiration for the crew dressed in white duck.

Old Marceau went home.

He would have quickly returned had he observed a dripping sailor, who had considerable resemblance to the trim looking chap who went out as the skipper of the Fancy, watch him well away and then stroll over to a young lady in white, under a wide hat.

"Joby, I'm glad," said the white figure.

"I'm glad you'r glad."

"You won't race again, will you?"

"Onless I see the skipper in white duck talkin' soft to you."

"I didn't."

"He did."

"Oh you old Jealous; that was pa's plasterer, Tim Fagan. Now!"

"By mighty, I dunno but you'r right." And they strolled down the street to see the wheelbarrow races, greasy pig and what the posters denominated smaller sports. But Joby turned his face and softly whispered to himself:

"By the horn spoon! If I'd a known that was Tim in his plaster overhalls, I'd a lost the race sure as guns."

Wars and Rumors of Wars.

Napoleon Bonaparte Marceau came into the log cabin just before the shadow fell upon the noon-mark on the window sill. He set a pot of beans on the hearth from the hook in the fireplace, and hung in its stead an empty rye-and-Indian kettle, threw in some scrap lead, oiled the bullet molds and began cleaning a rather bright-looking flint-lock made in part by his own hands.

His wife protested against such rude interference with dinner:

"Bone Marceau I am sick of the smell of venison. So you needn't go. I'll cook no more of it in this house."

"Cook it outdoor then," responded Marceau.

Soon he had run a pouch full of bullets, which he hurriedly trimmed, and then ran a pocket half full to make sure of a good supply. Seizing a piece of smoked venison and the half of a corn meal cake which he wrapped in a piece of linen and shoved into a pocket, he picked up the musket, slinging powder horn and shot bag over his neck, and with gun at "shoulder arms" he strode out the door giving the wife this admonition which contained the first intimation of his intentions:

"Be keerful of the fires and milk the cow reg'lar. The

British is goin' fer to try to take the Harbor and we are goin' to show 'em once more how we ben fitten at gineral trainin'," and he was off to the war without romance, or goodby formalities, except a dignified military salute to his wife at a point where the path disappeared in the woods.

The wife called to him to "take no risks and watch out for them pesky Hessians and hired Ingens."

"Lord!" she exclaimed, "war and blood at our very doors." Then she sat down and cried over her loneliness and the distress of the country.

The next day in the midst of her spinning she was startled by the distant boom of a cannon, then another and another.

"The alarm guns!" she exclaimed.

Mrs. Marceau had not seen the maneuverings of the British fleet on the lake as her husband had, and the report of the alarm guns was the first intimation she had had of real war. Slipping on a woolen shawl she ran a mile to the nearest neighbor, Mrs. Lane. That good woman was mounted on a wagon looking soutaward as if sight would pierce the hills and woods and reveal the scene of the battle. Her husband, too, had gone at his country's call, but less informally than had Marceau. The two women whispered and watched in the direction of the battle. A dense cloud of smoke lifted itself slowly above the hills and treetops on the opposite shore, and more certainly located the struggle in human blood. The cannonading ceased as suddenly as it began and the two women clutched each other's clothing as each looked inquiringly at the other. There was a faint rattle of the discharge of small arms and for a moment silence. Then the louder report of a musket reached their ears.

"Bar-r-ng!" it said, if translated into talk.

"I fear their powder is gone," said the elder of the women, "that was neither a musket nor a cannon, unless it be the last bit of powder fired from a cannon."

"That was my husband's musket," replied Mrs. Marceau positively. "That was my husband's 'Old Utica,' as he calls it, and he says it takes a ball a third heavier than any gun west of Albany," she added with a show of pride.

No sleep came to their eyes that night as they revolved over and over the probability of success or defeat. Hoping and praying, over and again they imagined the experiences of widowhood, and trembled at the least noise lest it were the approach of the British. Morning came and with it the duties of the day, but work was out of the question. The children were kept indoors. The clank of oars caught their attention and to the shore they cautiously made their way.

"Thank God! we are not widows," fervently spoke Mrs. Lane.

A boat was approaching and instead of Hessians the husbands of the frightened women landed.

Marceau's hand was wrapped in the linen that had served the purpose of a napkin when he had hastily seized his lunch.

"Got a ball through my hand," he half apologized, "but if twan't pizened I shan't be bothered long. It came after the bugle sounded to 'cease firing,' but I gin 'em one salute from 'Old Utica,' as they pulled out to the ship in their boats, just to make 'em bail as they hed to for I seen a splinter leave her starn."

"Yes," said the neighbor, "you made a bigger hole in the boat than they did in your hand, I'll warn you. Show 'em your venison, Sargeant," and he saluted his superior officer, who had received a promotion without having been enrolled in the service. The venison was produced and a hole almost closed was first exhibited and then turned to the opposite side, where a little of the substance had been cut away showing the end of a pointed ball which had lodged there while the piece was still in his pocket.

"Tough meat that, or I wouldn't be here," coldly remarked Marceau, and the women shuddered at a realizing sense of the horrors of war not yet revealed to them by the injured hand which had not been uncovered.

In the excitement of the return, a young man dressed in a semi-military uniform was nearly forgotten.

"Here Bill," suddenly called Lane, "come up and get acquainted with the women. This is my woman, and this Bone's wife—Leftenant Vaughan, who has come hum with us to larn what the Britishers 'll do next."

The young man bowed low, saluted, and the ladies courtesied.

"Ye don't look real pert and well, stranger," remarked Mrs. Lane. "Come in and sit by. I've some wheat flour and I will have some white biscuits and honey. Don't 'pear to me as you are any great eater, anyway."

The young boatswain said he "didn't mind," if the men were going in. "Lieutenant" was a title facetiously applied by Lane to make his introduction more impressive.

"You see," began Lane as they entered the house, "me and Marceau got to the barracks just afore the Britishers made Horse Island, and the leftenant here wants to get the lay of the land hereabouts. Bein's Bone and me see the redcoats pintin' that way when we ware scoutin on our own book"——

"Avast, there!" growled Marceau, "you'r losin' yer beariin's agin, neighbor. The leftenant is a great angler and bein' a little offen his feed he's about to take pot luck with us and recooperate by way of huntin' 'n fishin'."

"And if that don't help you jest try bleedin'," added Lane with a wink that ran from the cords of his neck up into his scalp. It was a sly dig at Marceau who needlessly suffered shame at receiving a wound.

"Better try a steepin' of plantain leaves and snake-root fust," timidly put in Mrs. Marceau at a pause.

Lords of creation! In the interest of truth it must be stated that the two settlers had been smuggling pot and pearl ashes into Canada when they learned of the approach of the British fleet, long before the alarm guns were sounded.

And the sickly lieutenant! He was sound as a bullet, and had been sent out as a scout to reconnoiter the lake shore and find the enemy's vantage points on the St. Lawrence River. He was an acknowledged marksman with the fowling piece, or a 24-pounder from the deck of the flagship. He was a studious sailor, too, not content with steering his trick, he passed his watch below studying some old prints on the science of navigation.

Vaughan passed many days coasting the shores between Gravelly Point and Stony Point, searching out harbors and shoals, watching for the enemy, and reporting his occasional presence at the River into which he ventured a few times, always in company with his new-found friends, Lane and Marceau.

When he returned to the post at Sackets Harbor, General Wilkinson had superceded General Brown and was formulating a plan to descend the River with an overwhelming force and capture Montreal. To this plan Vaughan, who had been promoted to sailing-master, made strenuous objections when he was called into the conference.

The officers studied a rude map which Vaughan had hastily drawn from a knowledge gained while scouting on the lake shore.

"What you have been accustomed to call an island, here," explained the scout, "is really a peninsula connected with the main shore by a strip of land about ten yards wide. I pulled my boat across it often and found a most excellent harbor inside. Outside in the lake lies an island well toward Gravelly Point, which contains a fine harbor almost landlocked. Its form is that of a basin and we have named it Basin Harbor. That point would make a very desirable rendezvous for the expedition to Montreal, if that is the campaign upon which you are determined. The harbor can be reached from the east side in small boats, but not by those of deep draft. The approach from the lake side is dangerous for those unacquainted with these waters. One must hug the north shore close to find a deep channel leading right into the harbor. Not far out lie treacherous rocky ledges, but once clear of these shoals the harbor will protect the whole fleet."

Our fleet was assembled at Grenadier Island on the 27th, at least such of our boats as survived a gale which set in during the night Of this expedition Dr. Hough wrote:

At this late season of the year, when with no other enemy but the weather, it would seem the extremity of folly to attempt the navigation of the lake in open boats, from the peril arising from sudden tempests, it was decided to pass the enemy's fleet and army, and descend upon Montreal, allowing the enemy the privilege of attacking on his own territory in both front and rear, with an intimate knowledge of the country and its resources, and every advantage that a skillful commander could have desired, had the selection of circumstances been left to him. Viewed in its proper light, the expedition may be justly considered an outrage upon reason and common sense, and justly entitled to the odium which has been attached to it.

On the 26th of October, at noon, orders were issued for the heavy, light and flying artillery, commanded by Colonels Porter, Eustis and Macomb, and the fourth brigade, commanded by Brigadier-General Swartwout, of the infantry, to embark, and proceed immediately to Basin Harbor, in Grenadier Island. At six p. m. the whole embarked, and put off with a favorable wind, the transports mostly consisting of scows, Durham boats, common lake sail boats, and bateaux, containing besides officers and soldiers, ordnance, ammunition, hospital stores, baggage, and two months' provisions for the troops. An unpardonable negligence was evinced during these and the following movements, in the custody and safe keeping of the supplies, immense quantities of which were ultimately lost.

There was a deficiency of experienced pilots, and the men in the boats were mostly unaccustomed to their management, either in good or bad weather, and particularly in a dark night, and, in passing points of land where they were unacquainted with the soundings and currents, and at a season when sudden and violent tempests are liable to arise without warning.

The wind and weather favored until one o'clock a. m., when the boats appeared to be much scattered; some had landed on Pillar Point, and Point Peninsula; some had entered Chaumont Bay, and other inlets; others had landed on Cherry, Stony and Horse islands, and others stood off for Kingston, where one boat, with an officer and ten men, is said to have arrived in safety. Several boats landed on Long Island, in British territory, and some safely reached their destination at Basin Harbor. At half past two the wind shifted nearly ahead, and blew fresh from the lake, by which many boats got in the rear, and discovering lights on the shore, attempted to reach them, in which some succeeded. It soon began to rain, and the wind increased to a gale, in which the boats and scows which had landed, were drifted and beaten on the shore, which in some places was rough and rocky, while others, still on the lake, made the first point of land they could discover to save themselves. The morning disclosed a scene of desolation truly distressing. The shores of the islands and main land were strewn with broken and sunken boats, and the day was spent in unloading such as could be reached, and in endeavoring to save such perishable articles as could be found, the gale continuing through that day and the following night. On the 18th, the wind having abated, several boats were got off from the rocks, and arrived at Basin Harbor, but on the next day the storm increased, and several boats that had attempted to gain their rendezvous, were driven back upon the shores. On the 20th the day was favorable, and many of the sound boats reached Basin Harbor.

The brigades of Generals Brown, Boyd and Covington which had encamped at Henderson Harbor, arrived at Grenadier Island on the 20th. Of the flotilla that had left Sackets Harbor, fifteen large boats were entirely lost, many others, with several scows were much damaged, and a large quantity of bread was destroyed. The troops remained encamped on the island until the first of November, engaged in repairing the boats and making preparations to descend the St. Lawrence. The weather meanwhile continued stormy, and snow fell to the depth of ten inches. Many of the regulars were from the southern states, and unaccustomed to the severity of a northern winter, and in this expedition, especially at a later period, suffered extremely from the rigor of the climate, which produced a frightful mortality among them.

On the 28th, 196 of the sick were put on board of a schooner and sent to Sackets Harbor. Wilkinson arrived on the 27th, and finding a large body still in the rear, wrecked or stranded, returned to Sackets Harbor to order a supply of winter clothing and shoes, for the troops on the island, some of whom were nearly destitute. He observed many fires of troops along the shore, but the wind was so violent that he could not communicate with them. On the 23d, Colonel Cole arrived with 200 men, of the 12th regiment, and sailed for the rendezvous, and the Growler was sent to Oswego for Colonels Randolph and Scott, who were expected there, and as many men as the vessel could carry. The general returned the same day to Grenadier Island and arrived off the island at eight in the evening, the weather continuing boisterous during this night and the day following, with frequent rains and heavy gales, so that a landing could not be effected until the 25th.

In the intervals of the gale, opportunities were watched to slip detachments of boats into the St. Lawrence, but so treacherous were the lulls of the tempest, that great peril was encountered in passing from Grenadier Island to Cape Vincent, a distance of nine miles. Many boats were driven ashore and much provisions and clothing were lost. General Brown was ordered to take command of the advance and post himself at French Creek, where the detachments were ordered to rendezvous. The Growler arrived at Grenadier Island on the 31st, with 220 men of the 20th regiment, and on the 2d of November, Chauncey took a position to protect the south channel, where it was apprehended the enemy would enter and occupy Fort Carleton, which, with some repairs, would have effectually commanded that channel, and compelled the American army to winter on Lake Ontario, or run the gauntlet under the batteries of Kingston. Perhaps no point on the river is so admirably adapted for a military post, as the head of Carleton Island, and it has been justly called the Gibralter of this passage.

So much for prosy history. General Brown's fleet was piloted from Grenadier Island to French Creek by Lane, Marceau and (now) Captain Vaughan, though the latter had been so far in the River on but one occasion, and that in the night. As they passed Bartlett's Point the general saw in that promontory the advantage of position, and a battery of three eighteen-pounders was landed, drawn up the hill, and left in command of Captain McPherson. Captain Vaughan was detailed as expert gunner, and the compliment to his marksmanship pleased him more than would a promotion to commodore of the fleet. His old friends, the smugglers, piloted the fleet into the bay at the mouth of French Creek, past Indian Point, where the west end of the bridge rests today, and up the stream to a point suitable for a camp of seven thousand men. The place once called Wilkinson's Point, is better known as the Hubbard House farm.

A sharp lookout was kept night and day at Bartlett Point, now Prospect Park, inasmuch as it was known that the enemy was lurking among these Thousand Islands, and his presence might not be discovered until he had reached an uncomfortable proximity. The two pilots coasted about in canoes acquainting themselves the better with the intricacies of the channels, big and little, deep and shallow, narrow and wide.

From the battery a wide sweep of vision was had up and down the River. The view directly across was limited by the dense growth of firs, balsams, pines and hemlocks which in places appeared rooted in the very granite foundations. Captain Vaughan, seated upon his gun, drank in the beauties of the scene with more than the appreciation of an ordinary soldier. Early frosts had tinted the leaves, and the fire red maple backed by the varied shades of green and gray gave back a sharp reflection in the still autumn day. From his elevated position the observer fell to noting the apparent regularity with which the dead pines were stationed like so many silent sentinels, an effect the more striking, the greater the distance.

Was that the wing of a huge bird in a dead tamarack?

Captain Vaughan, standing up, brought a long spyglass into range and gazed intently at a tall tree which had been blasted by lightning. The air was not in motion, yet he distinctly saw the fluttering as of a flag in the breeze, a full league down stream. Hastily dispatching a messenger for the pilots he noted the appearance and disappearance of the phenomenal signal which Nature in her freakiest mood could not simulate.

The pilots arrived from the camp at Wilkinson's Point and were saluted in an unconcerned manner, and then drawn back upon a knoll a little apart from the gun crews.

The captain pointed northerly toward the dead tree which towered above the oaks and maples.

"Now, watch."

A white flag was waved from horizon to horizon, and in the blaze of sunlight its outline became very distinct.

"One, two, three," counted the captain, and after a pause the signalling was resumed. This time the observers counted two, then, after another pause, one.

The gaze of the pilots met in a half-quizzical expression.

"Cap'n, we've seen that kind of flutterin' before, eh! Marceau, when we crossed with the last load of potash"——

"Shet up, Lane! Do you want the hull revenue ossifers arter yer onworthy skin? The feller up a tree's got a pardner, Cap'n. Want to see him? Then promise me and Lane a promotion to admirals of this fleet and I'll show you tother one, besides"——

"Nonsense, men," interrupted the captain, "if you know anything more of this fluttering business than I can guess, out with it for this is no time for sport."

"Right you are," said Lane, and he swept the upstream shore with his hand as Marceau brought his gaze to a standstill.

"There's his pardner," said the pilot as a signal was waved from another treetop on the Canadian shore.

"'Bout six mild apart in these ratholes, Cap'n. Lots on 'em between Kingston and Windmill Pint."

"Yes," offered Lane, "the smugglers used to think the customs house officers climbed trees to warn the approach of Yankee potash peddlers."

"Well?"

"Well, it means ther's a gunboat or two, or maybe a brig, or two or three schooners betwixt them air treetops, sir, and if you want the feller in the tree just give the order. Me an' Lane'll bring him!"

"Yes—no," responded the captain, still watching for the reappearance of the signals. "It may be we can read as well as they, after we learn."

The pilots disagreed as to the exact location of the tree first observed by Captain Vaughan, and after obtaining permission, paddled off with the current to make a closer inspection of the locality. After going a mile or more they located the tree more accurately, and then remembered that near it a palisade opened into a large bay of shallow water. These palisades would screen a tall mast from any but an open view at each end of the channel.

Suddenly Marceau touched Lane on the shoulder and pointed significantly to the main channel to the northward.
Both paddles rested in the water.

A brig flying the British jack lay moored to a precipitous cliff whither she had been helplessly carried by the current when the wind gave out. Towering above a low island could be seen some masts. A small boat, approaching the brig, seemed filled with soldiers.

The pilots were for the moment seized with the "fever." Their first move was to turn about and paddle back under the friendly shadow of an island, and then exchanging ideas by a mere glance, they set their paddles deep and shot the canoe back toward the rendezvous with long, rapid strokes. At the shore they parted, Lane to report to General Wilkinson, the other to Captain Vaughan.

The latter met Marceau in the brush for he had seen the pilots returning and suspected the enemy's presence. After receiving the news he walked back to his gun, which he patted affectionately after carefully noting that everything was in readiness.

"This expedition is a fool job, Marceau," he half mused, "for here are we with the enemy in front, in the rear and on the flank. This is defending our country but not saving it as I look at it."

"Be that as it may," replied the other, "ther'll be business on this hill before another sun sets if the wind blows anythink short of a hurricane."

A sighing in the pines suggested wind, but as yet the water had not been disturbed. The glassy surface gave back a smiling reflection of Nature's face, and birds in their flight shot downward at their own shadows expecting to make the acquaintance of another of their kind.

"Another night-breeze from the north," suggested Marceau, who had been watching the moving branches. "The brig will make our acquaintance before many hours, eh! captain?"

The captain did not heed. He was sweeping the bay, the shore and the islands with his glass and making mental calculations. The battery was masked behind some fallen trees and a good breastwork of logs. The enemy undoubtedly had information of the concentration of the troops in French Creek, but they would seek in vain for the battery, even if they suspected its presence on the promontory.

The northerly breeze stiffened and one after another of the beautiful reflections were erased from the face of the waters as a frown swept over them with the increasing ripple. Fled like a smile from a happy face was the enchanted isles which a moment before had been suspended trees downward in a beautiful mirror set in a frame of gneiss, or forming a rich fringe as from a beautiful garment. The horror of war was spreading over all the landscape as occasional clouds obscured the sun.

Was yonder ship growing out of the rocks, coming up out of the deep, or gracefully alighting from an aerial flight? Another and yet another seemed to launch from the mass of green and gold leaves into which the descending sun shot his brightest rays as a beacon light reveals an otherwise hidden danger.

Vaughan warned the sentinel, he gave the alarm, messengers were dispatched to General Wilkinson's camp, and then the drums sounded the long roll. Seemingly out of the rocky walls the fleet of the enemy came in a light breeze. Two brigs, two schooners, and several smaller boats loaded with infantry, he numbered. The pilots were evidently unacquainted with the waters they were navigating. A brig led the fleet and it was evident that it was the purpose to go into the mouth of the creek and give the Americans battle on shore, and under the protection of the naval guns.

Charcoal fires were lighted at the battery, and wires were kept hot for firing the powder which was put into the muzzle of the guns in bags. Captain Vaughan had made his reputation at Sackets Harbor when he effectually captained a thirty-two pounder loaded with twenty-fours, the deficiency made up by wrapping carpets around the balls. He was determined that the set of sun should not see the luster of his prowess dimmed on this occasion. The fleet approached Bartlett Point and as the largest brig began to ware off Captain McPherson gave the order to give battle—Captain Vaughan to fire first. He waited until the masts appeared as one and gave the word to his mate to fire. Marceau already had the red hot wire in hand and at the word ran it down the vent.

The gun spoke.

The commander, watching through the glass, saw all three shots fall short of the mark.

The invaders were evidently surprised at a salute from that quarter, for the brig luffed as if her master wished to make a closer acquaintance, and then poured out a broadside at the hill. Their aim was bad and the balls whistled high over the battery, while the otherwise silent woods mockingly echoed and re-echoed the roar. By this time Captain Vaughan was again ready for another shot. As before, he took careful aim and when the smoke cleared away he had the poor consolation of seeing the brig's sails torn and the rigging evidently cut. The other gunners now paid their respects to the second brig and the schooners. They shot away some of the rigging, but no serious damage was done until the brig which gave the invitation to battle was nearly hove to the third time to present a broadside.

"Now," said Vaughan to his mate, "get everything ready for a quick fire and I will do some damage if powder will carry a ball."

The brig bore up to the wind and just as the yards swung around and the masts had barely passed out of range, the captain sighted his piece. Marceau already stood by him with the red hot wires and at the word pushed one down the vent and pierced the bag of powder which had been rammed down behind two balls. The single bag of powder had been re-inforced by near half a bag which Marceau had quietly poured in, contrary to orders.

The gun roared, the promontory trembled, the smoke hid the enemy.

"Well done," shouted Commander McPherson, as the black veil lifted. "Vaughan you have brought down the foremast."

This called out a cheer from the entire battery, as well as a broadside from the second brig. The fleet had been describing a circle in the maneuver, as they wore around and stood away from the creek, when saluted from the masked battery. The small boats of infantry were ineffectual at that range, and made but one move to land. That was effectually checked by the battery's concentrating its fire upon the schooner that attempted to protect them in landing. The fleet was now close together and afforded an excellent mark, but as the balls tore their sails and rigging they realized the superiority of the position of the Americans and with the small boats towed the disabled brig out, and soon the whole fleet dropped down stream with the current, the wind having died away.

During this half-hour's engagement the troops in the

camp had been drawn up in dress parade and stood at rest as idle spectators. Most of them had been under fire, but not a few of them winced as the balls from the port side of the brig whistled over their heads and fell harmless into the marsh or woods beyond. Only a few of them were favored with a view of the battle. The enemy was less fortunate for it is evident that they did not know the exact location of the rendezvous as their aim was much too high. Two men at the battery were wounded and one was killed outright. The British loss was not ascertained, and great or small the world loses nothing by lack of information regarding the numerical slaughter in human blood on this or any other occasion.

Night came.

The pickets were redoubled about the rendezvous, and every preparation was made to guard against a surprise by land and water. The exultant Americans knew full well the temper of the race with which they had to deal, and past experiences had taught them that this foe, though defeated, was not vanquished. The night was cool, with just wind enough moving to tumble against the shores a slight swell which falling with a regular cadence lulled the soldier into sleep, or set him tumbling on his hemlock couch as the nervous system was tuned to harmony or otherwise. Often in the darkness the sentinels were startled by the mournful cry of the loon, or the sharp beating of his wings and feet upon the water in his clumsy attempts at flight.

The morning came.

Sunrise at the Thousand Islands! The first faint glow of light in the east foreshadowed the glories of the dawn of a beautiful day. Not so much as a breath of air moved, for the very wind was awed into silence as the mellow light turned to a soft pink and then to a glowing red which spread over that portion of the horizon. In the water the changing tints were copied as upon the painter's canvas. Long shadows crept away from the trees crowning the rocky bluffs whose sides the water lazily lapped, just as a fond mother awakens a child with a caress lest it be startled at a too sudden awakening. The air, laden with the resinous odors of cone-bearing trees, seemed to have gained volume during the night, and the soldiers from the far south declared they could fairly taste it. Here and there a shining maskalonge, the Frenchman's "long-face," shot out of his native element and fell back with a resounding splash upon the still surface. A V-shaped flock of geese, led by the regular "quonk, quonk," of a sober old pilot gander, roused company after company of the sleeping troopers who contentedly fell back again at the responsive "la-la-lunk," of the mother goose as they pressed their flight southward. The sentries forgot their beats, and looking over the rude ramparts become lost in admiration of the miraculous birth of another day. The morning star faded. The halo of morn was reinforced with bright rays shooting upward and outward by companies like glistening spears behind a golden battlement which a fleecy cloud caught up in bold reflection as if to mirror the splendors of a glorious sunrise for Nature's own admiration. Higher and yet higher shot the pinnacles of light. Shorter and shorter drew the shadows. Fainter and fainter became the red glow, and lighter and lighter became the leafy caverns that a moment ago seemed dark and impenetrable. The glistening channels, which lay scattered about like silver threads, shot away into the more intricate and all but inaccessible labyrinths of this mighty cathedral not of man's construction.

A flock of whistle-wings tacked upstream, and a sober crane slowly beat the air as with legs stretched back like a pair of paddles, and neck closely coiled, he sought his favorite wading place where frogs were greenest, and little fish most venturesome. Upward and upward climbed the streaks of red and white and yellow, until as with a myriad of golded wires the sun's disk was slowly lifted into the horizon whence he was to cut his way across the heavens in the ceaseless pursuit of ever-fleeting dawn.

The reveille!

Bugle sound and beat of drum recalls the stern fact that in the midst of these peaceful solitudes War, red-handed, blood-thirsty War, stalks abroad in a reign of terror.

When the disabled fleet drifted out of range of the battery, Commander McPherson was anxious to follow and overtaking them complete the victory. Not for a moment did he think that the policy of General Wilkinson would be otherwise. His anxiety was the possibility that his command would be ordered to remain, and others be sent out in their stead. No orders were issued and the attacking party departed as unmolested as though going for an outing.

"Vaughan," suggested the commander, when it was certain no orders for the pursuit were to issue, "what do you say to following the fleet and bringing them back as prizes?"

"Get thee behind me, Satan," quoted Vaughan. "It's a shame to let them slip away just when we had them fairly caught. But its a sample of what the 'reglars' are made of. Marceau and Lane would capture the hull bilin' on 'em with a canoe! I tell you its a fool expedition, this."

The men parted and did not meet until the next forenoon. Vaughan and the two pilots stood upon the crude breastworks and passed a spyglass from eye to eye.

Marceau spoke first: "Thet thare's no dead pine. Dead pines don't travel fur, and that one's opened a hand's width and whats onusual its got a mate follying at prezackly the same gait! Its a couple of topmasts a-loomin aloft the island, and we'll hev more celebratin' afore long, sir."

Vaughan motioned to McPherson, who took the glass but failed to verify the pilot's discovery, which in no wise disconcerted that worthy, who rather felt his superiority over the officer.

Lane took a long look and without removing the glass announced that there were "four dead pines walkin' up the crick, now."

Just then the bowsprit of the first schooner, for there was no doubt about it now, pushed out of a rocky cleft, and in a few moments the lately used up fleet was seen advancing to renew the combat. McPherson gave his men a few words of encouragement and then instructed the gunners to hold their fire until the enemy attacked. The fleet was short one brig on this occasion, a fact which Vaughan noted with some inward self-praise. The schooners led the brig by gunshot distance, and approaching boldly to the steep bluffs set a couple of twelve-pounders to sounding taps at the clear sky above. The battery returned with a concerted volcano of hell-fire and shot which cut some of the running rigging, and some of the sails drooped. This evidently disconcerted the schooners for they immediately fell back to the protection of the larger guns of the brig. The slight breeze was dying out and after firing a few random shots the fleet retreated as it had on the night previous.

No attempt was made to follow the enemy down the River, and camp at Wilkinson's Point was not broken until three days later. The soldiers suffered from want of shoes and winter clothing, and besides every man of them had intelligence to foresee the disaster which subsequently befell the expedition at Chrysler's Field.

At the battle of Bartlett Point two Americans were killed and four were wounded. McPherson was promoted to a captaincy, which office he had held by brevet, and Captain Vaughan was given command of the schooner Julia, whose successful cruising forms the subject of another chapter.

THE STORY OF TOM GARNET.

Ever since that period when man reared on his hind legs and walked, romance has been signally united with war. One of the most touching anecdotes of the second war with England is related of a hero of the Army of the North, as that arm on Lake Ontario and the St. Lawrence border was designated.

Tom Garnet was the son of an English farmer, living about forty miles from Liverpool. He chose a partner for life, and was sent not long after marriage with an ox cart laden with wheat to Liverpool, to exchange for furniture and an outfit, but was seized on the streets by a press gang, and despite his entreaties and resistance, was taken on board a frigate, about to sail for the East Indies, his cart and oxen remaining in the street, and himself unable to relieve anxieties at home by a single word of explanation.

During seven long weary years, he was detained abroad, without an opportunity of exchanging letters with his family, or of knowing whether those most dear were dead or alive. At length, he was paid off and set on shore at Liverpool. Sunburnt by tropical heat, and haggard from hard service, he was so changed that his best friends would hardly have known him. He had carefully saved his earnings, and having shunned the vices that sailors too often acquire, he had with him a considerable sum, for a man of his station, with which he was fondly hoping to gladden the hearts of loved ones at home—if perchance they were still living. As night approached, fearing to call at an inn, lest his dress and appearance should excite suspicion that he might be a deserter from the fleet, he crept into a nook under a stack of straw, and spent the night. In the morning, there was a dense fog, and not knowing the course he should take, he fell in with another press gang, and was again carried on board a vessel about to sail for the South American Coast. After some years, finding an opportunity, he escaped, crossed the Andes, and at length, reaching an Atlantic port, he enlisted for a few months in an American ship, which soon brought him to the United States.

His crew was detailed for service on Lake Ontario, and he arrived at Sackets Harbor in the fall of 1812, and joined the crew of the brig Oneida under Lieutenant Woolsey. During twenty years he had been unable to gain the first word from home. He was of a kind, cheerful and obliging disposition, was strictly temperate, used no profane language, and was made captain of the forecastle, from the entire confidence that was placed in his capacity and fidelity. In short, Tom Garnet was the universal favorite of the brig, and both officers and men became strongly attached to him for his kindness of heart, intelligence and moral worth.

On the morning before the fleet of Commodore Chauncey sailed to meet the enemy near Kingston, Tom related to his comrades a dream he had the night before, in which his wife appeared to him as a disembodied spirit in Heaven, with a son, whom he had never seen, and told him he would soon join them. His story was treated with levity; but the calm and serious earnestness with which he related it, and the evident conviction he had as to the premonition, checked hilarity. He proceeded to divide his wardrobe among his companions, and gave instructions about the disposal of the little property he possessed, as one about to die; yet his cheerfulness and alacrity were unabated; although he evidently believed in the presentiment he had expressed, he seemed exhilarated in the welcome prospect of meeting the long-lost and dear partner of early hopes.

The fleet sailed and engaged the enemy's batteries in the harbor of Kingston, the first shot from which was a nine-pound ball, which crossed the deck of the Oneida, and passed through the body of Tom Garnet at his post. He fell instantly dead, with the same smile upon his countenance which habit had impressed.

EARLY SMUGGLING.

A company of infantry, under Captain Bennet, and of twenty-three artillerymen, under Lieutenant Cross, were stationed at Sackets Harbor in 1808, and early in March, 1809, two detachments of militia (forty-five men), from Colonel Paul Stickney's regiment, were drawn out, twenty of whom were stationed on the St. Lawrence at Gravelly Point, now Cape Vincent, opposite Kingston, and the remainder at Antwerp on the Oswegatchie road, where several routes united. The embargo had the effect of lowering the price of grain, by interrupting the commerce by which it was exported, while from the same cause it enormously increased the price of potash, which all new woody countries produce, and which the embargo prevented from reaching England, except indirectly by way of Canada. This afforded a temptation too strong for the honesty of great numbers, who, notwithstanding the vigilance of the revenue officers were very successful. This article rose to $300 to $320 per ton in Montreal, from whence it could be exported without obstruction to England ; and as there then existed in Canada no law against its importation into the country, the only difficulty to meet was an evasion or open defiance of our own laws. Potash was brought from the interior counties, and even from New York to this frontier, and temporary roads were beaten through the forest in the winter time, by those engaged in this illegal traffic. Among these was the "embargo road," from the Black River, near Brownville, to near French Creek, which for a season became a great thoroughfare for smugglers.

Previous to the calling out of the militia detachments above mentioned, Mr. Hart Massey had seized fifty-four barrels of pot and pearl ashes, and twenty barrels of pork near Cape Vincent, which property was openly rescued and carried off by a force of fifty or sixty armed men, with many sleighs from Kingston.

Under date of March 14, 1809, the collector at Sackets Harbor made the following complaint to the Treasury Department :

Nature has furnished the smugglers with the firmest ice that was ever known on this frontier. There is scarcely a place from the Oswegatchie to Sandy Creek, a distance of 110 miles, but that the ice is good. Sleighs pass at Sackets Harbor ten miles from shore, and all the force I can raise is not sufficient to stop them. They appear determined to evade the laws at the risk of their lives. More particularly at Oswegatchie, I am informed, they have entered into a combination not to entertain, nor even suffer any other force to be stationed in that vicinity, and their threats are handed out, that if I, or any other officer should come there again, they will take a raw hide to them, which they declare they have prepared for that purpose. These threats don't terrify me. I only mention them to let you know their unprincipled determination. The regular troops, and the inhabitants at that station, have a mutual understanding. If the troops that are there, are not called away, it will be in vain to send any more, without sending enough to overpower them and the inhabitants.

The militia, stationed on the Oswegatchie, are thirty miles this way from the post, at the place where the roads branch off to various parts of St. Lawrence County. [Antwerp.] The people in the vicinity of their station are hostile and refuse to accommodate them with anything, even to admit them into their houses. They are in a suffering condition, and the snow is three feet deep. I shall go to their assistance soon, and furnish them with such things as they are in want of, to keep them from suffering. They are poorly armed, without blankets or cooking utensils, or even without shelter, except hemlock boughs, but, notwithstanding their distressed situation, they stop the illicit trade on that road. It is with difficulty that I get any assistance for the conveyance of property to the public store. If I have not armed men with me, the inhabitants will assemble in the night and take the property from me. There are some who wish to support the laws, but they are so unpopular that they shrink from their duty. My life and the lives of my deputies are threatened daily; what will be the fate of us, God only knows.

This open and bold defiance of laws, was not entirely due

to a mercenary spirit, but to political rancor and a practical opposition to a law which they declared unconstitutional and void. An open defiance to the law was attempted at Oswego, in the summer of 1808, it is said, in part, by citizens of Jefferson County, which was boldly planned but poorly executed.

One morning about ten boats with sixty armed men, entered that harbor, and from an intimation that was given by one of their number, it was learned that they designed to forcibly seize a quantity of flour that had been detained by the collector, Mr. Burt, or to use their own language, "to clear out the place or burn it." A message was at once sent to hasten on a company of dragoons at Onondaga, who arrived within half a dozen miles and encamped. Learning that the hour of 11 p. m. was agreed upon for a "scrape," the detachment was hastened forward, and arrived a few minutes before the signal was given. Hearing the music of the approaching company, the insolent marauders instantly fled to the woods, leaving their boats in charge of the collector. The great price to which ashes arose led for a short time to extensive clearings for this object as labor was far better rewarded in this, than in the ordinary pursuits of husbandry. On the first of March, 1809, the embargo gave place to a non-intercourse law, which expired in May, 1810. On the fourth of April, 1812, an embargo was again laid, which rendered renewed vigilance necessary; but this time a more efficient system of means was at hand.

In May, 1812, the Lord Nelson, a British schooner, bound for Niagara, and laden with flour and merchandise from Kingston, being found in American waters in the lake, was captured by Woolsey, brought into Sackets Harbor and condemned as a lawful prize. Among the goods taken and offered at auction was a quantity of plate, jewelry, wearing apparel and household articles of rich materials, belonging to a lady of Queenstown, newly married, but not on board; and these articles of great intrinsic value, were inestimably precious to the owner, as family relics and keepsakes. These, Commodore Woolsey, with true courtesy, proposed to restore, and the suggestion was seconded by the hearty acclamation of his gallant sailors, who offered to relinquish their claim; but others, from sordid and illiberal motives, insisted that the sale should go on, and undertook to compete in the bids, which gradually arose to three, four and five hundred dollars. At this moment, the gallant Woolsey, determined not to be baffled in his design, suddenly raised his bid to five thousand, which at once ended the contest, amid the cheers of his men, and to the discomfit of his opponents. The property, he promptly forwarded to the owner, and the government sanctioned his course by discharging him from the obligation.

THE WAR SCARE.

War having been for years anticipated, was declared June 18, 1812, by a vote of 79 to 49 in the house, and of 19 to 15 in the senate; Silas Stow then represented this district and voted in the negative. The event was first announced in a letter from Governor Tompkins to Brigadier-General Jacob Brown, of the militia, dated June 23, in which he was empowered to re-inforce Colonel Bellinger, with the militia of Lewis, Jefferson and St. Lawrence counties, and to arm and equip them at the state arsenals at Russell and Watertown, if occasion required. Colonel Benedict, of DeKalb, St. Lawrence County, was ordered to turn out immediately to guard the frontiers from Ogdensburg to St. Regis. In reply, General Brown urged the speedy forwarding of arms and munitions, and that a force should be posted at Cape Vincent and Ogdensburg, which could be concentrated at a few hours' notice, should decisive measures be necessary. This letter contained the following sentiments:

"Your Excellency will bear in mind, that this is a very new country; that the population is light, and generally poor, though very respectable for so new a country, and that, if any more men are called from their homes, the crops which now promise a very abundant harvest must perish on the ground. I mention this to your Excellency, as the county expects it at my hands, and much more than my feeble abilities can accomplish; but no considerations of this nature shall deter me for a moment from calling out every man in the county, if its defense requires it, though, for the present, I must hope that the force coming on, will render such a measures unnecessary. I pray God that our government will act with decision and energy which becomes a gallant people."

On the first announcement of war, some families hastily prepared to leave the country, to which they were impelled in part by fugitives of the same class from St. Lawrence County, and so terror stricken were some, that they hastily fled into the back settlements, spreading consternation on their way, and leaving their houses open to any who might choose to enter. But to the credit of the county the number of these timid ones was comparatively small, and several who had removed returned. The fear of Indian massacre, which the memories of the revolution suggested, was in general the impelling cause, although they could scarcely define the source from whence these dreaded marauders would come, or adduce a consistent argument to justify their apprehension. After a time, confidence began to return, until at length some settler ventured to cross the river by night, to call upon an old acquaintance. These visits gradually became more common, and by the time the war ended, old acquaintances had already been renewed; the river was crossed by daylight, and as often as there was occasion—and, in short, they found that although legally enemies, they were still friends.

The news of the war had scarcely reached this frontier, when hostilities were begun in a small way, by Abner Hubbard, a revolutionary soldier, who, without authority, and with only the aid of a man and a boy, made a descent upon Fort Carleton, near Cape Vincent, and, without firing a gun, took the garrison, consisting of three invalid men and two women, prisoners. The next day a boat was sent to the island for the stores, and the buildings were afterwards burned. This proceeding being known at Kingston, an attempt was made to detain a citizen from Brownville, who was in town on commercial business, but being forewarned by a friend he escaped. On the 29th of April, a fleet of trading vessels, that had been caught at Ogdensburg, and were attempting to ascend the river to the lake, were pursued by a party of provincial militia. Two of the vessels, the Sophia and Island Packet, were burned near Morristown, and the remainder returned in great confusion to Ogdensburg, where they created the greatest alarm. On the second of July, the scouts of General Brown brought in a man, found between Indian River and the St. Lawrence, who was taken for a spy, but proved to be an American and confirmed the account of the burning of the vessels, stating that there were about thirty persons aboard, mostly families moving; and that the most of their effects were burned. It was apprehended that the enemy were about to fortify the islands, and thus command the river. A few days before the news of war was received, a large quantity of small arms was forwarded by the governor to this frontier, consisting of two thousand muskets, and a corresponding quantity of munitions, which were mostly sent on to the Russell Arsenal, in St. Lawrence county, escorted by the detachment from Lewis County. A considerable body of militia from Jefferson County, was assembled at Cape Vincent, together with a portion of the force of Colonel Bellinger, as it was considered advisable to keep Kingston in as great a state of alarm as possible. At this point was the great naval station of the enemy, where for one or two years armed vessels had been building, and from whence alone an attack could be reasonably expected. It was apprehended that an attempt would be made by the British, to destroy or take our vessels at Ogdensburg, and the Oneida, Lord Nelson, and other vessels at Sackets Harbor. To be in readiness for any attack, the governor was importuned to forward cannon from the state arsenals, and the assurance was given that a good account would be rendered of the enemy, should they attempt any expedition to our shores. On the 11th of July a rumor was spread that Lieutenant Woolsey, with the brig Oneida, had been taken by the enemy, which brought General Brown to the Harbor, but the report proved groundless. There had arrived two brass nine-pounders, but no nine-pound shot.

FIRST BATTLE AT SACKETS HARBOR.

On Sunday, the 19th of July, 1812, Captain Woolsey, of the Oneida, discovered from the mast head of his brig, five sail of the enemy beating up the harbor, viz: the Royal George, 24 guns; the Seneca, 18; Prince Regent, 22; Earl of Moira, 20; and Simcoe. The Oneida attempted to gain the lake, but failing, returned, and was moored outside of the point, where the ship house stood, with one broadside of nine guns to the enemy, while the others were taken out and hastily placed on a breastwork on the shore, near which, on the day previous, a 32-pounder (intended for the Oneida, but found too heavy) had been mounted on a pivot, upon a mound about six feet high. Alarm guns were fired, and expresses sent to call in the neighboring militia, who did not, however, arrive in time to render assistance, but who, in the course of the day, came in to the number of 3,000. The British had, early in the morning, captured a boat laden with flour from Cape Vincent, and the crew was set on shore, and sent with the message "that all they wanted was the brig Oneida, and the Lord Nelson (a vessel taken a little before for a violation of the revenue), and that they would burn the village if there was a single shot fired at them."

The enemy had been misinformed about the defenses of the place, and especially of the 32-pounder, and supposed there was nothing to be feared in the way of ordnance. The force at that time in town was, besides the crew of the Oneida, the regiment of Colonel Bellinger, a volunteer company of artillery under Captain Camp, and a few militia. Captain Woolsey, leaving his brig in charge of a lieutenant, took the general command on shore, the 32-pounder being in charge of Mr. William Vaughan, sailing master, and the other guns under that of Captain Camp. There were no shot in town larger than 24-pound balls, which were used (with the aid of patches formed of carpets), in the 32-pounder.

By the time these arrangements were made, the enemy had arrived within gun shot, nearly in front of the battery, when the action was begun, the first shot being from the 32-pounder on the mound; upon which a shout of laughter was heard from the fleet, at the supposed imbecile attempt at resistance. The fire was returned briskly, and continued for two hours, all of the enemy's balls but one or two, falling against the rocks at the foot of the bluff, where our force was stationed. One ball fell near by, and plowed up the ground for some distance. It was caught up just when it had spent its force, by a man who came running in and shouting that he had "caught them out;" and so it proved, for from its commanding position, it was seen that our big gun had every advantage, and that several of its shots told with effect.

Towards the close of the action, as the Royal George, the flagship, was wearing to give another broadside, a 24-pound shot struck her stern, and raked her whole length, killing eight men, and doing much damage. Upon this the signal of retreat was given, and the whole fleet bore away for Kingston without ceremony. At this, the band on shore struck up the national tune of Yankee Doodle, and the troops, who had through the whole affair behaved like veterans, sent up three cheers of victory. The shots from our battery had broken their chests of medicines, their fore top-gallant mast, and their vessels in a dozen places, while the enemy broke nothing but —the Sabbath. In a letter to the governer of July 24th, General Brown attributed the success of the day to the gallant spirit of Woolsey, Bellinger and Camp, in their respective capacities, and especially to the nice shots of the 32-pounder.

Mr. Vaughan, who pointed and fired this piece, claimed the honor of having fired the first hostile gun in the war. One of the men at this gun, named Julius Torry, a negro, better known as Black Julius, and a great favorite in the camp, served at his post with remarkable activity and courage. As there was no opportunity for the use of small arms, the greater part of the troops who were drawn up, were passive spectators of the engagement.

CAPTURE OF GANANOQUE.

On the night of the 20th of September, an expedition was dispatched from Sackets Harbor, which is thus described by General Brown, in his report to the governor:

At a time when my force was the lightest, and a very considerable alarm prevailed for the safety of that port, I fitted out a secret expedition under the command of that excellent officer, Captain Forsyth, against Gananoqui, a small British post, twenty miles below Kingston, with the view of capturing some of the enemy's ammunition, of which we were and are greatly in want, and of alarming them as much as possible for their own safety. My order was executed by Captain Forsyth, as became an officer and a soldier, and Captain McNitt and Lieutenant Brown and Ensigns Hawkins and Johnson, of the militia, who volunteered on the expedition, are reported to me by Captain Forsyth as deserving the highest praise for their cool, intrepid valor and good conduct. There was not a man but did his duty. Captain Forsyth landed in open day, two miles above the village; his whole force amounting to ninety-five. At three-quarters of a mile he met two horsemen, one of whom was probably shot, the other fled to the village, where Captain Forsyth found on his arrival the enemy drawn up in order of battle, 110 strong, and upon his approach they commenced a heavy fire upon him, but over. He rushed immediately on, without firing, until within 100 yards, when his party made a few deliberate shots, then rushed on, and broke the enemy, drove them across a bridge, which, for his better security, Captain Forsyth broke up. He had one man killed and one wounded. The loss of the enemy, in killed, Captain Forsyth has declined stating, but from the best information I can collect from the party, it was from ten to fifteen. Twelve prisoners were taken, 3,000 ball cartridges and 41 muskets. There were in the king's store about 150 barrels of provisions, and as there were no boats to bring it away it was consumed by fire, together with the store. Private property was held sacred. To the soldiers on this expedition, I have presented the public property taken, as a reward for their valor and good conduct. I wish your excellency to approbate or disapprobate this my donation to these brave men. Your excellency must bear in mind, that with my very little brigade, or at best a part of that at Oswego, I have been put upon the defense of this northern frontier, from St. Regis to near Oswego. The men that I have the honor to command, have done and suffered much for the militia; their clothes generally were in tatters and they are poor men. They can not clothe themselves in this region for $6.66 per month, and it is not in human nature that these men can endure a winter campaign in this climate thus clad. I can not believe that these men would leave me; it would grieve me if they should; but it is a stain upon our national character, that the citizen soldier of this country should be worse paid and provided for, than any other class among us.

REDOUBTABLE KINGSTON.

Commodore Chauncey having taken a station near the False Ducks fell in with the Royal George, 26 guns, and chased her into the bay of Quinte, where she was lost in the night. On the morning of the 10th, he took a small schooner, which he burned, having got sight of the Royal George which he followed into Kingston harbor and engaged her and the batteries an hour and forty-five minutes, but finding these stronger than anticipated, night coming on and a gale of wind blowing in, he stood off and anchored. In the morning the wind continued so strong in shore that he thought it imprudent to hazard an attack, and beat out and soon fell in with the Simcoe, and chased her over a reef of rocks, but so disabled her with shot, that she sank before getting alongside of the dock.

On the morning of the 10th, he took a large schooner from Niagara bound in, and the next morning sent down the prize under convoy of the Growler, past Kingston, to induce the ship to follow, but without success. The night of the 11th was boisterous; on the 13th was a severe snow storm, and on the 14th it continued to snow fast, but little wind. The remainder of this cruise we give in the language of Commodore Chauncey, in a letter to the governor:

"The Growler sent the prize in, and stood in for the

Ducks, where he had orders to join me. Near the Ducks, he fell in with the Earl of Moira, convoying the sloop Elizabeth from York to Kingston. Sailing Master Mix, who commanded the Growler, run down in a very gallant manner and took possession of the Elizabeth within two miles of the ship, and brought her in. I immediately weighed and stood for Kingston in hopes to cut her off, but the elements were against me again, for I scarcely had left the harbor before it blew a gale of wind, and snowed so thick that we frequently could not see a mile. We, however, persevered to the great danger of the vessels and lives of the crews. On the 14th we got sight of the Earl of Moira entering Kingston harbor, but it blowing a gale of wind, we concluded not to follow, and after beating about almost all that day, I made the signal for all the squadron to bear for this place, where we arrived on the same evening. During these two short cruises we captured three vessels, two have arrived, one we burned, a fourth was so injured that she sunk, and we learn from one who came in the flags yesterday, that the Royal George was so much injured that she had to haul on shore to keep from sinking, having received several shots between wind and weather, several guns disabled, and a number of persons killed or wounded, besides considerable injury (though not intentional) to the town. Amongst the prisoners is Captain Brock of the 29th regiment, and a relative of the late General Brock, who was returning from York with part of the baggage of his deceased friend. Our loss was trifling; one man killed and four wounded, two of the latter by the bursting of a gun on board of the Pert, the commander of which vessel, Mr. Arundell, was knocked overboard and drowned. The damage done to the rigging and sails not much, and a few shots in the hulls of one of the vessels, but the injury from which was soon repaired. The Gov. Tompkins, Hamilton, Conquest and Growler are now blockading the vessels in Kingston. I am now taking on board guns and stores for Niagara, for which place I shall sail the first wind, in company with the Julia, Pert, Fair American, Ontario and Scourge, and I am in great hopes that I shall fall in with the Prince Regent, or some of the royal family which are cruising about York. Had we been one month sooner we could have taken every town on this lake in three weeks, but the season is now so tempestuous that I am apprehensive we can not do much more this winter. I am however, ready to co-operate with the army, and our officers and men are anxious to be engaged."

This brilliant maneuver conferred great credit upon those engaged, and called public attention to the operations on this frontier, as likely to afford a theater for deeds of valor, that would confer honor upon the American name. The spirited engagement in Kingston harbor has been compared, by Cooper, to the assault upon Tripoli, in our previous war with the Barbary States, to which it was not in the least inferior, due allowance being made for the comparative force employed. The fact of the Royal George, which was by much the largest vessel that had then been built on our inland waters, retiring before the Oneida, has been ascribed, by Cooper, to her not being properly officered. The British had not then made their drafts upon the royal navy for the service of the lakes.

The bones of the Oneida lie in the French Creek Bay in sight of one of her conquests. The people of Clayton should be patriotic enough to see that what is left of her should be suitably preserved just as the government has already taken steps to preserve the Constitution immortalized in the poem as "Old Ironsides."

SECOND BATTLE AT SACKETS HARBOR.

The descent upon York provoked the resentment of the enemy, who, knowing that Sackets Harbor had been weakened by the withdrawal of troops to the Niagara, planned an attack upon the former, well knowing that the capture or destruction of the vessels there building, and the stores collected, would at once give them the supremacy in the campaign, and effectually suppress any further offensive operations of the Americans for some time.

Sackets Harbor was at this time but poorly prepared for defense. Fort Tompkins, occupying the site of the present residence of the commanding officer of the station, was manned by about two hundred dismounted dragoons, under Colonel Backus, a detachment of forty or fifty artillerists, under Lieutenant Ketchum, and seventy or eighty infantry invalids, recruits and parts of companies. A little east of the village was Fort Volunteer, a slight work that had been chiefly erected by a company of exempts. General Dearborn had written to Brigadier-General Brown, to assume the command and make provisions for a defense, which letter was not answered from motives of delicacy toward Colonel Backus, but preparations were made for resistence, if required.

Between the village and Horse Island, a mile distant, was a thin wood that had been partly cut over, and was filled with brush, logs and stumps. Opposite the island was a clearing of about four acres, and the island itself, which embraces twenty-nine acres, and lies at the entrance of the bay, was covered with a growth of timber, and at that time connected with the main land by a bar that afforded a crossing, nearly or quite dry. The beach opposite was composed, then as now, of a ridge of gravel, which at that time made a natural breastwork, four or five feet high. A short distance back and further south on the shore, a strip of woods extended, which had been obstructed as much as possible several days previous, by felling trees in every direction.

The enemy having made preparations at Kingston for an attack, embarked 1,200 men, under Sir George Prevost, on the evening of May 27th, on board the ships Wolfe, a new vessel of 24 guns; the Royal George, 24 guns; the brig Earl of Moira, 18 guns; and the schooners Prince Regent, Simcoe and Seneca, mounting each several guns; two gun boats, and about forty barges under Sir James L. Yeo; and on the following morning (Friday, May 28th) appeared in the offing, having been discovered by the schooner Lady of the Lake, that had been cruising on the lake to watch the motions of the enemy.

As this vessel came in, signal guns were fired, and upon her arrival Colonel Backus dispatched an express to General Brown, who, since the expiration of his six months' term, had been residing on his farm in Brownville, eight miles from the harbor. He immediately repaired to that place, and issued summary orders for rallying the neighboring militia, and preparing the place for defense. Alarm guns were fired and dragoons dispatched in every direction to hasten the arrival of succor, and especially that of Colonel Tuttle, who was known to be advancing with several hundred regulars. No landing was attempted by the enemy on the 28th, their attention being drawn off by a fleet of American barges from Oswego, of which twelve were taken, their crews having fled to the woods, and seven, by outsailing the enemy got safely into port, thus increasing the disposable force of General Brown. These recruits proved to be a part of a regiment of infantry under Colonel Aspinwall, on his way by water from Oswego to Sackets Harbor, who did not discover the enemy until he was doubling Six Town Point. As the route of those that landed was very circuitous, they did not arrive until nine o'clock in the evening.

The militia soon began to assemble, and as fast as they arrived they were armed and sent to Horse Island, which was the point at which the enemy was expected to land. The number that came in during the day was about 600, fresh from their homes, and without discipline, experience or organization, and although not wanting in patriotism or courage, yet lacked that assurance which an acquaintance with military affairs can alone confer. These, with about 300 regulars and 100 of Aspinwall's party fatigued with their day's march, comprised the force by which the enemy were to be opposed.

The night was spent by General Brown in making dipositions for the attack which circumstances rendered highly probable would be made where the militia had been posted. The shore for most of the way between this place and the village is an abrupt precipice, fifteen or twenty feet high; and the fleet to land above the village, must have to pass the batteries on shore and would require a favorable wind. During the night the enemy landed about forty Indians under Lieutenant Anderson on the main land in Henderson bay with the view of attacking the rear of the militia, and towards morning the militia were withdrawn from the island to the shore opposite. Camp fires had been built along the shore early in the evening, but these were ordered to be put out.

About 400 militia with a six-pounder, under Colonel Mills, of the Albany volunteers, were stationed near the shore opposite the island with orders to reserve their fire until the enemy should approach within pistol shot. The remainder of the militia under Colonel Gershom Tuttle, were posted in the edge of the woods back of the clearing, and Colonel Backus with his dismounted dragoons was stationed in the skirt of the woods near the village with orders to advance through the woods towards Horse 'sland the moment it was known that the enemy had landed. Colonel Aspinwall with his men was posted to the left of Backus, and the artillerists under Lieutenant Ketchum were stationed in Fort Tompkins, with no other than a 32-pounder mounted on a pivot. The militia on the shore were directed that, in case of being driven from their position, they should fall back into the woods and annoy the right flank of the enemy as he advanced towards the town. Colonel Tuttle was directed in the same event to attack their rear and destroy their boats. The night was spent in making these arrangements and all parties anxiously awaited the approach of day.

The morning of the 29th dawned beautifully clear and calm. Not a breath of air ruffled the placid surface of the lake, and there existed that peculiar state of density and uniformity in the atmosphere, in which sounds are propagated to a great distance, as is sometimes noticed before a storm; and the report of small arms in the action which followed, was heard with remarkable distinctness on the hills in Rutland; while the discharge of cannon echoed clear and far over the country, to d'stances since unparalleled, and was heard through Lewis and even in Oneida County. This very naturally excited throughout the country the greatest anxiety and alarm and the solicitude of families for the fate of fathers, husbands and sons, who had been hastily summoned from home, was such as could scarcely endure the suspense which it occasioned.

The calm prevented the enemy from bringing their vessels to co-operate in the attack, and was one of the causes that influenced their subsequent retreat. As soon as it was light, the enemy was seen approaching in thirty-three large boats under cover of gunboats, directing their course to the outside of the island, where they landed and formed without opposition; but in crossing the bar that connected it with the main land they encountered a galling fire and lost several in killed and wounded, which they subsequently carried off. As the landing was being effected, the heavy gun in Fort Tompkins was brought to bear with considerable effect upon the enemy's column.

The fire of the militia was at first well directed and deadly and was answered by discharges of musketry and by two small cannon loaded with grape shot; but Colonel Mills, who was stationed a short distance towards the village with his cannon fell early in the engagement, and his death, with the unaccustomed whistling of balls that cut down the branches of the trees around them, struck with terror the inexperienced militia and without waiting to return the fire or recover from the panic, they turned and fled towards the town in the greatest confusion. This retreat was not entirely general. Captain Samuel McNitt, who had been stationed with his company on the extreme left of the flanking party of the militia, not noticing the movements of his comrades, continued his firing after some moments longer, and before he was aware he found himself and his party alone and in danger of being cut off by the enemy. General Brown finding himself nearly alone with no support but this company, retired towards the village, directing those that could be rallied to annoy the advancing column of the enemy as much as possible. The enemy, having gained the beach and dispersed the militia, formed in good order and marched towards the town.

They were soon met by the troops of Colonel Backus, who had advanced to dispute their progress and who gallantly encountered and returned their fire, retiring slowly before them through the half cleared woods. General Brown had succeeded in rallying about a hundred militia with the aid of Caleb Westcott, a citizen, and others, and had joined the detachment of Backus; but at this juncture, happening to look towards the shipyard, he was surprised to see huge volumes of smoke issuing from the storehouses that contained the spoils of York. Not knowing but that the enemy might have gained his rear, he hastened to the spot and ascertained that the disastrous panic of the militia had been communicated to those in charge and a report had reached Lieutenant Chauncey of the navy that all was lost, and upon the faith of this rumor he had given orders to fire the buildings, an act which the most extreme and desperate issue of affairs could alone justify. Learning the cause of the conflagration and somewhat relieved by the knowledge that the enemy were still but on one side, he returned, giving directions to Lieutenant Ketchum in Fort Tompkins to hold that post as long as the flames would permit. The regulars of Colonel Backus felt their courage renewed upon learning the nature of the accident that had given a natural alarm, and continued steadily to oppose the advance of the enemy who had now gained the clearing next the village. Very soon after Colonel Backus fell mortally wounded and was borne off the field; his troops taking possession of some log barracks and continuing their resistance.

The enemy had throughout evinced great courage and coolness and were under the immediate command of Captain

Gray, of the quartermaster-general's department, who was advancing in front of the ranks and walking backwards waving his sword for his troops to follow, and shouting, "Come on, boys; the day is ours! Remember York!" when he suddenly fell wounded and immediately expired.

At this moment the signal for retreat was given from the fleet and the enemy hastily retreated to their boats. This retreat is said to have been in part caused by hearing a report of small arms on the right from the rallied militia, but which the enemy mistook for a reinforcement of 450 regulars which they had learned was advancing under Colonel Tuttle, and was then within a mile of the place. Their arrival would at once put an end to the contest by giving us the advantage of numbers. The enemy on their retreat removed a part of their wounded, and having re-embarked, they at about 10 o'clock sent a flag demanding a surrender of the place which they had been unable to capture and were of course refused. They, however, were promised that decent attention should be paid to the dead and humane treatment to the wounded. They shortly after sent another flag requesting to send surgeons to their wounded, which was denied, as they still seemed not to have abandoned the attack and were laying by in their barges, but shortly after they put off to the fleet which lay about five miles from the town, and made sail for Kingston. Both Sir George Prevost and Sir James Yeo are said to have landed during the engagement.

The loss of the British was 150 in killed and wounded; 25 of their privates were found dead, 2 captains and 20 privates were wounded and including the wounded, 2 captains, 1 ensign and 32 privates were taken prisoners. Our loss was 150 killed, wounded and missing. The enemy took a few prisoners and one man was found killed and scalped in the woods by the Indians.

The flames of the burning stores were subdued as quickly as possible, but not till they had consumed half a million of dollars' worth of property. The ship Pike, then on the stocks, was saved. The prize schooner, the Duke of Gloucester, was saved by Lieutenant Talman, of the army, who boarded it, extinguishing the fire and brought her from under the flames of the store houses. This heroic conduct will be appreciated when it is known that a large quantity of gunpowder was on board. The schooners Fair American and Pert, cut their cables and retreated up the river and several of the guns on Navy Point were spiked. Had it not been for this disastrous mistake our success would have been complete. Colonel Backus survived eight days and hopes of his recovery were entertained, but blood-poison supervened.

PRIVATEERING.

On the 14th of July, 1813, the Neptune and Fox, the former a private armed boat under Captain Samuel Dixon, mounted with one six-pounder and one swivel, and manned by twenty-four volunteers, and the latter a public armed boat under Captain Dimock, with a detachment of twenty-one men from the 21st regiment of infantry under Lieutenants Burbank and Perry, sailed from Sackets Harbor with Letters of Marque from the deputy collector of the district for a cruise on the St. Lawrence. This privateering expedition was fitted out by M. W. Gilbert and others and had for its object the cutting off of a detachment of the enemy's boats that were expected up the river laden with stores. After touching at Cape Vincent and French Creek, they selected on the morning of the 17th a quiet nook in a creek among the Thousand Islands, where they landed for muster and review; and the morning being particularly pleasant, they employed themselves in drying and putting in complete order their arms and ammunition and cleaning out their boats, while a small boat of each was sent out for intelligence, which returned without gaining any news. At 9 p. m. they hauled from the shore, manned a guard boat to prevent surprise, and sent Lieutenant Hawkins to Ogdensburg for intelligence; and at 5 p. m. Messrs. Baldwin and Campbell arrived with news. At 9 they left Cranberry Creek and at 4 a. m. of the 18th saw a brigade of British bateaux convoyed by his majesty's gunboat, the Spitfire, lying at Simmond's Landing, preparing to sail for Kingston. Upon this, they pushed in for shore and so completely surprised them that very few of the enemy escaped. The fifteen bateaux and the gunboat were at once seized without a shot being fired on either side. Previous to the attack Lieutenant Perry, of the 9th, and Sergeant James, of Forsyth's company, with 27 volunteers were landed in Cranberry Creek in Alexandria, and at 11 sixty-nine prisoners were sent off to the harbor under guard of 15 men of the 21st in charge of Lieutenant Burbank. The Spitfire was armed with a 12-pound carronade and 14 men with a large quantity of military stores. The bateaux had 270 barrels of pork and 270 bags of pilot bread which was landed on the 20th to prevent spoiling, and a request to the neighboring inhabitants for assistance was sent out, which brought in a few militia, who, however, mostly left the same night. At sunrise on the 21st the enemy to the number of 250, with four gunboats and one or two transports, were discovered in the creek; these were met by thirty men and attacked while landing, twenty more being stationed in different places to prevent their approach. A cannonade commenced and was kept up some time; two of the enemy's boats were so injured from our fire that most of their crews were compelled to leave them and to cut flags from the shore to stop the holes. At 6 a. m. the enemy retired to their boats and sent a flag with the demand of surrender to save the effusion of blood, which was instantly rejected and the firing recommenced. It appeared that this was but an expedient to gain time, as the enemy hastily retreated carrying their dead and wounded. Their loss must have been considerable from the quantity of blood seen where they embarked. Our loss was three killed and wounded. After the action trees were felled across the road and creek to prevent a new attack, and on the afternoon of the next day reinforcements arrived, the boats which had been scuttled were repaired and on the 23d they left for Sackets Harbor, where they arrived on the 27th. While passing Tibbet's Point they encountered the Earl of Moira, were pursued and hit several times by her shot, but not captured. The gunboat and several bateaux were sunk without consulting Captains Dimick or Dixon and the owners ultimately lost most that was gained by the expedition.

A RIOT.

The armaments of the small vessels were abandoned early in the season and they were used mostly as transports. On the first of May the frigate Superior (66 guns), built in eighty days, was launched, and the day after there occurred an incident which well nigh led to serious consequences. The ship carpenters and sailors having no interests in common with the soldiers had acquired a feeling of mutual hostility, and on this occasion there had been an unusual degree of convivial excess in celebrating the launch. A dragoon, being assaulted by two or three carpenters, fled for protection to a sentinel placed over a storehouse, and with the obstinacy and insolence of half drunken men, they were persisting in the pursuit in which one of their number was shot and the remainder fled. This at once led to the most intense excitement. The ship carpenters with axes and adzes hastily rallied with the sailors armed with boarding pikes and cutlasses, who, forming in a solid body, marched in pursuit of the sentinel. The troops were hastily formed in a hollow square around him and drawn up in the street, where they stood prepared to repel any attack, and the former had advanced to within a few yards and were yelling and brandishing their weapons in the wildest frenzy of rage, when Eckford, Chauncey and Brown hastened to the spot, threw themselves between the parties, and by a well-timed and judicious appeal checked the advance and soon persuaded the carpenters to desist on the assurance that the sentinel should be impartially tried and suitably punished if convicted. He was taken to Watertown, an examination held and he was sent to a distant station to be out of their reach.

The Mohawk and Jones were still on the stocks, the armament of which, as well as that of the Superior, must be transported through Wood Creek and Oswego river, as the roads through the Black River valley were nearly impassable with mud. This the enemy well knew and were also informed that the rigging and armament of these vessels was on its way to Oswego. To possess these supplies would be equivalent to the destruction of our squadron, as without them the new ships could not appear on the lake, nor could the fleet of the previous year venture out in the presence of the greatly increased naval armament of the enemy with the slightest hopes of success. This descent upon Oswego was therefore planned with great foresight and had its execution been as successful as its conception was bold and masterly, the beam of fortune must have preponderated with the British and the results of this campaign might have been as disastrous as those of the previous year had been disgraceful to the American arms. This fact being remembered will enable us to duly estimate the value of the services which rescued this property from the grasp of the enemy, and secured the defeat of the detachment that was sent in quest of it, as completely as could have been possible.

TRANSPORTING NAVAL STORES.

Oswego had not been occupied by regular troops since the revolution, and Colonel Mitchel had arrived at Sackets Harbor April 30th, with four companies of heavy and one of light artillery served as infantry. Of cannon the fort had but five old guns, three of which had lost their trunions. Platforms and pickets were repaired and the place was hastily put in as good a state of defense as possible, when the enemy appeared on the 5th of May with a force of four ships, three brigs and a number of gunboats. A cannonade was begun and returned with much spirit and a landing attempted, but not accomplished, when the enemy stood off from the

shore for better anchorage. One or two of the enemy's boats
were picked up and guards were stationed at various points
along the shore. At daybreak on the 6th the fleet again approached the village and after a fire of three hours landed six
hundred of DeWaterville's regiment, six hundred marines, two
companies of the Glengary corps and three hundred and fifty
seamen, who took possession of the public stores, burned the
old barracks and returned on board their fleet on the morning
of the seventh. The land forces were under General Drummond, and the fleet under Commodore Yeo.

The naval stores were then at Oswego Falls (now Fulton),
but Colonel Mitchel having retired in that direction destroying
the bridges and filling the roads with timber after him, the
enemy thought it inexpedient to follow and soon after the
fleet returned to its station near the Gallou Islands to blockade
the passage of the stores, which it was known must pass in
that vicinity. These stores, under the charge of Lieutenant
Woolsey and escorted by Major D. Appling, of first rifle regiment, with a company of one hundred and fifty men, left Oswego on the evening of the 28th of May in nineteen boats in
the hope of gaining Stony Creek unmolested, from whence
there would be but three miles of land carriage for the heavy
ordnance and stores to Henderson Harbor, twelve miles from
Sackets Harbor. The evening being dark and rainy, the brigade of boats rowed all night and at dawn on Sunday morning met a party of Oneida Indians under command of Lieutenant Hill, of the rifle regiment at Salmon River, and at
noon, May 29th, entered Sandy Creek, except one boat which
from the misfortune or treachery of its pilot fell into the hands
of the enemy. This boat contained one cable and two twenty-
four pounders, and from those on board the enemy learned
the particulars of the expedition and of the force by which it

was escorted. Upon entering Sandy Creek Lieutenant Woolsey sent an express to notify Commodore Chauncey of his arrival and couriers were dispatched in various directions to rally teams to get the stores removed by land to their destination. The boats were run up the south branch of the creek, till they grounded a distance of two miles from its mouth. The lake is here for a great distance bordered by a low ridge of sand hills, slightly wooded, behind which is a marsh with open ponds. Through this marsh, which is destitute of trees or bushes and at that time was partly flowed from high water, the two branches of Sandy Creek meander and unite but a few yards from their mouth, where then, as now. [1853] a solitary family dwelt.

On Monday morning a lookout boat in charge of Lieutenant Pierce discovered the enemy making for the creek and communicated the news to Lieutenant Woolsey who, at dawn dispatched messengers to call in the neighboring militia, and made hasty arrangements to meet the enemy who were seen soon after sunrise to enter the creek with three gunboats, three cutters and one gig and commenced a cannonade with a sixty-eight pounder in the direction of the flotilla of Lieutenant Woolsey, the masts of which were visible in the distance across a bend in the creek. These shots were directed in part against a thick wood that extended on the north side of the south branch to nearly half a mile below the boats in the edge of which, fronting the open marsh, the rifle company of Major Appling was concealed behind a brush and log fence entirely unobserved by the enemy. At nine o'clock Captain Harris, with a squadron of dragoons, and Captain Melvin, with a company of light artillery and two six-pounders, arrived. This reinforcement was directed to halt a short distance in rear of the boats as the force best calculated for a bush fight was already on the ground they could occupy with the best advantage. Meanwhile the cannon were posted in a position where they could be used with effect if necessary, and the fences thrown down that the dragoons might maneuver without obstruction. The enemy slowly advanced up the creek and landed on the south side, but finding it impossible to proceed, on account of the slimy condition of the marsh, they re-embarked and proceeded on to within about twenty rods of the woods, where they landed and formed on the north bank at a place now occupied by a storehouse and which afforded the first solid ground for marching. The advancing column, headed by Mr. Hoare, a midshipman of the British navy, had approached to within ten rods of the ambush, when, on a signal, the riflemen of Major Appling arose from their concealment and fired. Several fell dead and their leader fell pierced with eleven balls. So sudden and effectual was this movement that it threw the enemy into confusion, and after a fire of a few minutes, the order was given to charge, upon which the riflemen rushed forward with loud cheers, holding their rifles in the the position of charged bayonets. The result was the surrender of the enemy at discretion.

This was scarcely done, when the Indians, true to their character as savages, came furiously on, yelling and brandishing their weapons and were with the greatest difficulty prevented from murdering the disarmed prisoners, and, indeed, it has been generally believed that one or two British officers were mortally wounded after they had yielded. The enemy were commanded by Captains Popham and Spilsbury and their loss was nineteen killed, fifty wounded and 133 taken prisoners. A few landed on the south bank and fled, but were pursued, and not one escaped to report their defeat. Among the prisoners were 27 marines, 106 sailors, with two post captains, four lieutenants of the navy, one captain of marines, two lieutenants and two midshipmen. The captain of marines and one midshipman died of their wounds. Popham is said to have been an old acquaintance of Woolsey's and as he came forward to surrender his sword, the latter exclaimed:

"Why, Popham! what are you doing in this creek?"

After some indifferent reply and a survey of our force, he replied:

"Well, Woolsey, this is the first time I ever heard of riflemen charging bayonets!"

At the moment after the first fire the enemy had attempted to retreat, but the recoil of their heavy ordnance had forced the stern of their larger boats into the mud and they found it impossible. Upon this they attempted to throw overboard their armament and succeeded in getting out one brass piece, but were prevented from further mischief by our men. Our loss was one Indian killed and one rifleman wounded. On the morning of the battle Captain Smith was ordered on with 120 marines, and Colonel Mitchell, with 300 artillery and infantry, who did not arrive in time to participate in the engagement. The same was the case of the neighboring militia, who soon after arrived in great numbers.

The conduct of Lieutenants McIntosh, Calhoun, McFarland, Armstong and Smith, and of Ensign Austin, who were under Major Appling, was especially commended in his official reports of the engagement. The dead were buried, the prisoners marched to Sackets Harbor, measures were taken to erect shears for unloading the heavy freight and, at 5 p. m. Woolsey was relieved by Captain Ridgeley, whom Chauncey had sent for the purpose. The official report of Lieutenant Woolsey acknowledges the unremitted exertions of Lieutenant Pierce, Sailingmaster Vaughan and Midshipmen Hart, Mackey and Canton in the affair. The roads were then new and almost impassable and the labor of removing the guns, cables and rigging was one of no ordinary magnitude. There were, when the flotilla left Oswego, twenty-one long 32-pounders, ten 24-pounders, three 42-pounder carronades, ten cables and a quantity of shot and other articles. A cable and two guns had been lost in the boat that fell in with the enemy and the prizes taken in the creek were one 24-pounder, a 68-pound carronade, with several smaller cannon and a considerable amount of small arms and ammunition. Such was the industry displayed in this labor that on Thursday there remained nothing but one long cable, which it was found extremely difficult to load on any vehicle, as it could not be divided, and a sufficient number of teams could not be advantageously attached to it. In this dilemma the idea was suggested of bearing it upon the shoulders of men, and the proposal was cheerfully adopted by the citizens who had assembled to assist in these operations. They were accordingly arranged in the order of their stature and at the word of comr and shouldered the ponderous cable and took up their line of march for Sackets Harbor, about twenty miles distant, being as near together as they could conveniently walk. This novel procession passed by way of Ellis Village and Smithville and on the second day reached the Harbor. As they approached the town the sailors came out to meet them and with loud cheers relieved them of their burden and marched triumphantly into the village.

THE BLACK SNAKE.

The British fleet received large accessions to its naval force. The care that they evinced in the selection of officers for this lake indicates the importance they attached to its control, and the industry that both nations displayed in the fitting out of large vessels, seemed to portend a mighty struggle for its supremacy. There occurred, meanwhile, some operations on a minor scale that demand our notice. With the view of cutting off some of the detachments of boats that were ascending the St. Lawrence with supplies, Chauncey about the middle of June directed Lieutenant Francis H. Gregory to take three gigs with their crews and secrete himself among the Thousand Islands to watch for some opportunity to surprise and bring off or destroy some of these brigades of loaded boats.

This expedition consisted of Lieutenant Gregory, William Vaughan and Samuel Dixon, sailingmasters, and eighteen men, armed with rifles, pistols and cutlasses. They saw two brigades of boats passing up full of troops and too strong to attack, and another passing down and not worth taking. Gunboats were found stationed about once in six miles and a system of telegraphs erected on the heights, so that intelligence could be conveyed with great dispatch. On the 19th the party were laying close under the Canada shore, four miles below Alexandria Bay, and near Bald Island, when a gunboat was coming down under easy sail, but nearer the middle of the channel. Upon seeing the boats an officer with one or two men was sent in a skiff that was in tow to make inquiries of them, supposing them to be Canadians. Upon approaching,

Gregory hailed the strangers, demanding their surrender, which from necessity was obeyed; but those on board seeing the movement opened a fire, which was returned. The vessel was soon taken and found to be the Black Snake, or No. 9, Captain Landon, with one 18-pounder and 18 men, chiefly royal marines. The prize was taken in tow and when a mile and a half below French Creek was met by a British gunboat. Finding escape impossible the prisoners and small arms were taken out and their prize scuttled at the foot of Round Island. The enemy arrived soon after, but not being able to save it from sinking pursued Gregory's party several miles. Night coming on, he escaped, reached Grenadier Island late in the evening and the next day arrived safe at Sackets Harbor with his prisoners. The commodore in his official report warmly recommended Gregory, Vaughan and Dixon to the notice of the department for their activity, zeal and success in the cruise. Congress, by an act passed May 4, 1834, awarded Gregory and his men $3,000 for this service.

MINOR EVENTS.

On the 17th of September, 1812, General Brown, who had his confidence, addressed the following letter to the governor: The first and only official notice that I have received from my government of the renewal of offensive operations against Great Britain came to hand yesterday by the way of Ogdensburg. Would it not be advisable to establish a line of post horses by the way of Johnstown to Lowville and from thence to this place and Ogdensburg? Were I permitted it should be done forthwith. General Dodge advised me last week that he counted upon having 900 men embodied at Utica last Saturday and that these men would move to the frontiers with as little delay as possible; but I am yet to learn that they have marched or moved. I humbly trust that what it was in my power to do with the means at my command has been done, and that I am disposed to do what in me lies to prosecute this just and honorable war.

The inferiority of our fleet is thus related in Cooper's Naval History: "In the course of the autumn the Americans had increased their force to eleven sail, ten of which were the small schooners bought from the merchants and fitted with gunboat armaments, without quarters. In addition to the vessels already named, were the Ontario, Scourge, Fair American and Asp. Neither of the ten were fit to cruise, and an ordinary eighteen-gun brig ought to have been able to cope with them all in a good working breeze in close quarters. At long shot, however, and in smooth waters, they were not without a certain efficiency. As was proved in the end, in attacking batteries and in covering descents they were even found to be exceedingly serviceable."

At Sackets Harbor it was feared the British would cross on the ice. On the 9th of March, 1813, General Dearborn, who greatly feared a surprise, thus wrote to the secretary of war: I have not yet had the honor of a visit from Sir G. Prevost. His whole force is concentrated at Kingston, probably amounting to six or seven thousand, about three thousand of whom are regular troops. The ice is good and we expect him every day and every measure for preventing a surprise is in constant activity. The troops from Greenbush (upwards of 400) have arrived. I have heard nothing from Pike; he should have been here yesterday. I have sent three expresses to meet him; neither has returned. I have suspicions of the express employed by the quartermaster-general to convey the orders to Pike. The earliest measures were taken to convey a duplicate of his orders. By the 13th, the apprehensions of attack had nearly subsided, and General Dearborn again wrote: From the most recent and probable information I have obtained, I am induced to believe that Sir George Prevost thinks it is too late to attack this place. He undoubtedly meditated a coup-de-main against the shipping here. All the apprehension is now at Kingston. Sir George has visited York and Niagara and returned to Montreal. Several bodies of troops have passed up from Montreal; but such precautions have been taken to prevent their number being ascertained, as to render it impossible to form any accurate opinion of their forces, or even to imagine very nearly what they amount to. From various sources I am perfectly satisfied that they are not in sufficient force to attack this place knowing, as they do, that we have collected a fine body of troops from Greenbush and Plattsburg and that the militia have been called in. We are probably just strong enough on each side to defend, but not in sufficient force to hazard an offensive movement. The difference of attacking and being attacked, as it regards the contiguous posts of Kingston and Sackets Harbor, can not be estimated at less than three or four thousand men, arising from the circumstance of militia acting only on the defensive.

Brigade orders: The unoffending citizens of Canada are many of them our own countrymen, and the poor Canadians have been forced into the war. Their property, therefore, must be held sacred; and any soldier who shall so far neglect the honor of his profession as be to guilty of plundering the inhabitants, shall, if convicted, be punished with death.

But the commanding general assures the troops that should they capture a large quantity of public stores he will use his best endeavors to procure them a reward from his government.

On the 14th of June, 1813, Lieutenant Wolcott Chauncey received orders from Commodore Chauncey to proceed on a cruise, and having reached the vicinity of Presque Isle, in the schooner Lady of the Lake, on the morning of the 16th fell in with and captured the English schooner Lady Murray from Kingston bound for York, and laden with provisions, powder, shot and fixed ammunitions. One ensign and fifteen privates, belonging to the 41st and 104th regiments, were taken. The prize was taken into Sackets Harbor.

On the 2d of July a secret expedition was fitted out from Kingston, with the design of firing the Pike and the naval stores at Sackets Harbor in the night. On arriving at the isthmus of Point Peninsula they drew their boats out and concealed them in the bushes till circumstances might favor them, but a deserter from their number having escaped to Sackets Harbor, they returned back. Upon receiving intelligence of this, a force was sent to intercept the detachment, but without success.

The Sylph, pierced for 24 guns but carrying 20, and schooner-rigged, was built and ready for service in thirty-three days from the time her timber was growing.

On the night of May 25, 1814, Lieutenant Dudley with two guard boats fell in with three of the enemy's in the bay, who were hailed, but not being properly answered, were fired upon when the latter fled. A reinforcement was hastily obtained but nothing was seen or found of the enemy except six barrels of powder, slung in pairs to be carried on the shoulders of men, and doubtless intended to fire our vessels stealthily. This accounted for their hasty retreat when fired upon, for fear of accidental explosion. This insidious plan of the enemy could scarcely have succeeded, as, besides two lines of guard boats, all the approaches were secured by booms, and a marine guard boat and numerous sentinels were posted near. The guns of the Madison that was close to the stern of the Superior were kept loaded with canister and bags of musket balls, to rake under if necessary.

The Mohawk, a frigate of 44 guns, was launched at Sackets Harbor, having been but 34 days in building. The indomitable Mr. Henry Eckford, the energetic shipbuilder, who directed this department, acquired a large fortune in the war, but was subsequently reduced by some stock operations. He died at Constantinople, November 12, 1831, where for several years, he had been chief director of the dock yards in the Turkish Empire. No higher compliments to his talents could be paid than that of the sultan, who, in speaking of him said that America must be great, if it could spare such men as Eckford.

On the 9th of August, Abram Shoemaker, with his brother and a Mr. Sergeant, in a boat, bound from Oswego to Sackets Harbor, was attacked off Stony Point by a British barge, under a lieutenant of marines, and after a valiant resistance was captured. After securing the prize, the lieutenant sent all his men to join another boat's crew, except four, which number he deemed sufficient to secure her. Seizing a proper moment, and without waiting for a concerted signal, Shoemaker pushed the lieutenant overboard, knocked down a sailor, and, calling upon his comrades to help, soon found himself the master of the boat, but severely wounded by a cutlass. The movement being seen by the other boat, they were obliged to abandon their prize, but succeeded in reaching Sackets Harbor in a small boat.

Great apprehensions were felt for the safety of the Harbor, which led to an application to the executive for aid. Colonel Washington Irving, aid-de-camp to the governor, arrived at this station October 5, 1814, with orders to the commanding officer to make such requisitions on the militia as he might deem necessary. After consultation with Colonel Mitchell, General Collins called the militia, en masse, from the counties of Herkimer, Oneida, Lewis and Jefferson. The two former produced about 2,500 men, the latter not more than 400, which made the force at the harbor between five and six thousand men. Great difficulty was experienced from the want of suitable quarters for so great a body. Many were quartered in dwellings and barns, and from twenty to thirty were often assigned to a single room. The discomforts attending these accommodations very naturally excited uneasiness, and at the expiration of the draft, it was apprehended that the militia would be with difficulty prevented from going home, and that it would become necessary to supply their places with regulars. The apprehensions were not justified by the events that followed, and the militia were allowed to return home. Two frigates of the largest class, one on Navy Point, in Sackets Harbor, to be called the New Orleans, and another of the same class at Storr's Harbor, farther up the bay, to be called the Chippewa, were begun and their hulls partly completed, when the news of peace put a stop to the war.

Up the St. Lawrence, 1796.

Mr. Isaac Weld, an Irish refugee, as he was leaving Montreal in September, 1796, for a journey up the St. Lawrence, had as his first concern to provide a large tent and some camp equipage, buffalo skins, a store of dried provisions, kegs of brandy and wine, and, in short, to make every usual and necessary preparation for the journey. Except for about fifty miles, there were roads and scattered settlements at no great distance from each other all the way up to Kingston; but no one ever thought of going by land, as there would be great difficulty in hiring horses and in crossing streams without bridges, says Dr. Hough.

The bateaux were never laden until the boats had been got up the Lachine Rapids. Three men could take an empty boat of two tons up these first rapids, keeping as close as possible to the shore and using poles, oars and sails, as found most advantageous. It was a very laborious task; but from long observation they had been able to find places some times half a mile or in others two or three miles apart, where they could take breath. Each of these places the boatmen called "une pipe," because they were there allowed to fill their pipes, and this term had come to be a sort of itinerary measure, as, such a place is "three pipes off." The "pipe" was about equal on an average to three-quarters of an English mile.

The passage up the rapids was so tedious that travelers often proceeded on foot, by the roads along the north shore.

Coming up from Lower Canada in midsummer, by the tedious water passage, which had then been somewhat relieved by canals and locks for bateaux, he noticed, as he reached the level of lake navigation, enormous flocks of pigeons, "which during particular years come down from the northern regions in flights that it is marvellous to tell of."

Weld's description of the voyage to Kingston is as follows: The current of the St. Lawrence from Oswegatchie upwards is much more gentle than in other parts between Montreal and Lake Ontario, except only where the river is considerably dilated as at Lakes St. Louis and St. Frances; however, notwithstanding its being so gentle we did not advance more than twenty-five miles in the course of the day, owing to the numerous stops that we made, more from motives of pleasure than necessity. The evening was uncommonly fine and towards sunset a brisk gale sprang up, the conductor judged it advisable to take advantage of it and to continue the voyage all night, in order to make up for the time we had lost during the day.

We accordingly proceeded, but towards midnight the wind died away. This circumstance, however, did not alter the determination of the conductor. The men were ordered to the oars and notwithstanding they had labored hard during the preceding day and had no rest, yet they were kept closely at work until daybreak, except for one hour, during which they were allowed to stop to cook their provisions.

Where there is a gentle current as in this part of the river the Canadians will work at the oars many hours without intermission; they seem to think it no hardship to be employed in this instance the whole night: on the contrary, they plied as vigorously as if they had but just set out, singing merrily the whole time. The French Canadians have in general a good ear for music and sing duets with tolerable accuracy. They have one very favorite duet amongst them called the "rowing duet," which as they sing they mark time to with each stroke of the oar; indeed, when rowing in smooth water they mark the time of most of the airs they sing in the same manner.

About eight o'clock the next and eighth morning of our voyage, we entered the last before you come to that of Ontario, called The Lake of a Thousand Islands, on account of the multiplicity of them, which it contains.

Many of these islands are scarcely larger than a bateaux, and none of them, except such as are situated at the upper and lower extremities of the lake, appearing to me to contain more than fifteen English acres each. They are all covered with wood even to the smallest. The trees on these last are smaller in their growth, but the larger islands produce as fine timber as will be found on the main shores of the lake. Many of these islands are situated so closely together that it would be easy to throw a pebble from one to the other. Notwithstanding which circumstance, the passage between them is perfectly safe and commodious for bateaux and between some of them that are even thus close to each other is water sufficient for a frigate. The water is uncommonly clear as it is in every part of the river from Lake St. Francis upwards. Between that lake and the Utawas River downwards it is discolored, as I have before observed, by passing over beds of marl.

The shores of all these islands under our notice are rocky, most of them rise very boldly and some exhibit perpendicular masses of rock towards the water, upwards of twenty feet high. The scenery presented to view in passing between these islands is beautiful in the highest degree. Sometimes in passing through a narrow strait you find yourself in a basin, landlocked on every side, that appears to have no communication with the lake, except by the passage through which you have entered. You are looking about, perhaps, for an outlet to enable you to proceed, thinking at last to see some little channel which will just admit your bateaux—when suddenly an expanded sheet of water opens upon you, whose boundary is the horizon alone. Again in a few minutes, you find yourself land-locked, and again a spacious passage as suddenly presents itself; at other times, when in the middle of one of these basins, between a cluster of islands, a dozen different channels, like so many noble rivers, meet the eye, perhaps equally unexpectedly, and on each side the islands appear regularly retiring till they sink from the sight in the distance.

Every minute during the passage of this lake, the prospect varies. The numerous Indian hunting encampments on the different islands, with the smoke of their fires rising up between the trees, added considerably to the beauty of the scenery as we passed through it. The Lake of the Thousand Islands is twenty-five miles in length and about six in breadth. From its upper end to Kingston, at which we arrived early in the evening, the distance is fifteen miles.

The length of time required to ascend the River St. Lawrence, from Montreal to Kingston, is commonly found to be about seven days. If the wind should be strong and very favorable the passage may be performed in a less time; but should it, on the contrary, be adverse, and blow very strong, the passage will be protracted somewhat longer. An adverse, or favorable wind, however, seldom makes a difference of more

than three days in the length of the passage upwards, or in
each case it is necessary to work the bateaux along by means of
poles, for the greater part of the way. The passage downward
is performed in two or three days, according to the wind. The
current is so strong, that a contrary wind seldom lengthens
the passage in that direction more than a day.

Kingston, as seen by Mr. Weld, just before the beginning
of the present century, contained a fort, barracks for troops,
an Episcopal church, and about a hundred houses, mostly inhabited by persons who had emigrated from the United States
at the close of the Revolutionary war. Some of the houses
were of stone or brick, but for the most part they were of
wood.

From sixty to one hundred soldiers were usually quartered in the garrison. The town had a considerable amount
of trade, and was growing rapidly in size, the goods and
peltries of traders being here transferred from bateaux to
vessels. The principal merchants were mostly partners of
old-established houses in Montreal and Quebec, and the
stranger, especially if a British subject, was sure to meet a
most hospitable and friendly reception among them.

Kingston was then the principal station for shipbuilding
on the Lakes, and at that period, several decked merchant
vessels, schooners, and sloops, of from 50 to 200 tons each, and
numberless large sailing bateaux, were kept employed on Lake
Ontario. There were then no vessels larger than bateaux owned
on the south side of the Lake, and the British vessels that plied
between Kingston and Niagara, rarely touched at any other
place.

The heaviest item of ship-building at that period was iron,
which came from England, but great hopes were founded upon

the copper of the Lake Superior country, which was then known to exist, but had not yet been worked to much extent.

The established rate of passage across the Lake was then two guineas in the cabin, and one guinea in the steerage, including board. Freight was 36 shillings Sterling per ton, or nearly as much as then charged across the Atlantic.

Down the St. Lawrence, 1818.

John M. Duncan in 1818 descended the St. Lawrence, and recorded his observations. Another day or two might have been agreeably spent here, [at Kingston,] but October was closing upon me, and I feared that frost might set in, which would make traveling both difficult and disagreeable. It was, therefore, with pleasure that I learned that some bateaux were to go down the river the following morning, and I did not fail to be at the water side in time to secure a passage by them. * * * The Durham boats of the St. Lawrence are similar to those on the Mohawk. In smooth water they use a sail or oars, but are forced up the rapids by incessant and laborious exertions with the pole. They are generally navigated by natives of the United States. The one in which I sailed in May, was according to the information of the Captain, 62 feet in keel, and 11 feet 4 inches in beam. She carried about 26 tons, and drew only 28 inches of water. She had on board about 270 barrels of flour, which sunk her gunwale within a few inches of the water; and to defend us in passing through the rapids, a couple of stout planks, about a foot in breadth, were nailed along the sides; a precaution which, as we afterwards experienced, was no more than needful.

Bateaux are flat-bottomed boats, about half the size of the others, tapering to a point at each end, and so substantially constructed that they will endure a great deal of hard knocking on the channel without danger to the passengers. They do not sink so low in the water as the boats navigated by Canadian voyagers,—veterans who have been trained from their youth to the use of the paddle and the setting pole, and who know every channel, rock, and breaker, in the rapids, from the Long Sault to Montreal. If a traveler going down the River has his choice, let him by all means prefer the bateaux; it does not sail as fast as a Durham boat, and he may be a day longer in making the passage, but in ordinary cases he is far safer.

Passengers by either of these vessels must take with them a moderate supply of provisions, for it is not customary to go on shore except to sleep; and if the wind is ahead, four or five days may be spent between Kingston and Montreal. Going up the river is a far more tedious process. They should also be well provided, even in summer, with cloaks or other coverings, for the night dews on the rivers are excessively cold.

The bateaux sailed from Kingston with a favorable breeze, between ten and eleven in the forenoon, and while the wind lasted got on gallantly; but towards the afternoon we were almost becalmed in the Lake of a Thousand Isles, and our voyagers were compelled to tug away at the oar. We had four rowers, besides the conductor, who steered with a small paddle. The scenery of this Lake, as it is called, is very picturesque, but the succession of islands becomes at last tiresome, the more so that you find them take the wind out of the sail, and wofully retard your progress. I had made allowance for a reasonable proportion of exaggeration in its poetical name, but the Islands crowded upon each other in such numerous groups, and we were so long in getting clear of them, that I began at last to doubt whether there might be two thousand of them instead of one.

They are of all sizes; some of them bare rocks, a few feet square, others two or three miles long, and thickly wooded. Loch Lomond, with her two dozen islets, has long sheltered the manufacturers of the genuine peat reek from the scent of the Revenue officers; but this must be the very paradise of smugglers, should such a trade ever become profitable in Upper Canada—and a hopeless business it will be for excise men who are sent to ferret them out.

Towards evening it began to rain; but some of the company on board were more disagreeable than the weather. * * * * But for their presence, I could have endured the rain for an hour or two, to listen to the boat songs of the Canadian voyagers, which in the stillness of the night had a peculiar pleasing effect. They kept time to these songs as they rowed; and the splashing of the oars in the water, combined with the wildness of their cadence, gave a romantic character to our darksome voyage.

In most of the songs, two of the boatmen began the air, the other two sang a response, and then all united in the chorus. Their music might not have been thought extremely fine, by those whose skill in concords and chromatics forbids them to be gratified but on scientific principles. My convenient ignorance of those rules allowed me to reap undisturbed enjoyment from the voyagers' melodies, which like many upon Scotch airs, were singularly plaintive and pleasing.

Our conductor expected to have reached Brockville that evening, a small town about 59 miles below Kingston, but we began to be somewhat impatient to get on shore. The evening was so dark, that we could with difficulty distinguish even the shadowy outline of the river ; not a sound was heard around us but the echo of the voices of those on board, or the splash of the oars ; and we were gliding along with no other convictions of safety than what arose in firm confidence in our boatmen. About eight o'clock a twinkling light by the river's side broke upon our view ; we hailed the cheering spark, and urged the conductor to haul in to the bank, in the hope of obtaining lodgings. It was a farmer's house ; a crackling fire of pine logs blazed on the ample hearth, festoons of sliced apples for winter pies, hung around it to dry, and the comfortable kitchen contrasted most agreeably with our situation in the bateau in darkness and rain. The inmates made us welcome to their fireside, and although not much used to entertain strangers, very soon provided for us a most comfortable supper. Hot steaks, fried bacon and potatoes for those who preferred it, tea and toast, were served up with an alacrity that would have done credit to a regular inn. It scarcely needs to be added, that we enacted wonders with the knife and fork. When the time of retiring came, every bed in the house was surrendered for our use ; but finding that I could not participate in one, unless I accepted a bed-fellow, I preferred my box-coat and the floor.

About two o'clock next morning, we were aroused to resume our voyage. The boatmen before starting swallowed a plentiful allowance of soup thickened with meat and bread, very similar to what sailors call lobscoss ; the players fortified themselves for the water by an antiphogmatic of rum.

The wind had shifted during the night, and was now right ahead. It was a genuine American North-wester, and blew as if it were resolved to take the skin off our cheeks. The water froze upon the oars, as they rose above the surface; and I never appreciated better the comforts of a thick traveling coat, and a fur cap. Our boatmen had to row without intermission; and although they did not always pull very hard, they tugged away with amazing constancy. About nine o'clock in the morning, we reached Prescott, sixty-seven miles from Kingston.

Captivity of Mrs. Howe, 1755.

The narrative of Mrs. Jemima Howe's captivity was first published in a booklet, and later was popularized in the school readers of 80 years ago. The copy from which this is reproduced is characterized by the modified f for s in all instances except at the end of a word, as "fons."

As Messrs. Caleb Howe, Hilkiah Grout, and Benjamin Gaffield, who had been hoeing corn in the meadow, west of the river, were returning home a little before sunset to a place called Bridgman's Fort, they were fired upon by twelve Indians, who had ambushed their path. Howe was on horseback, with two young lads, his children, behind him. A ball, which broke through his thigh, brought him to the ground. His horse ran a few rods and fell likewise, and both the lads were taken. The Indians in their savage manner, coming up to Howe, pierced his body with a spear, tore off his scalp, stuck a hatchet in his head, and left him in this forlorn condition.

He was found alive the next morning after by a party of men from Fort Hinsdale; and being asked by one of the party whether he knew him, he answered, Yes, I know you all. These were his last words, though he did not expire until after his friends had arrived with him at Fort Hinsdale.

Grout was so fortunate as to escape unhurt, but Gaffield in the attempt to wade through the river which was indeed fordable at that time, was unfortunately drowned. Flushed with the success they had met here, the savages went directly to Bridgman's Fort. There was no man in it, and only three women and some children, Mrs. Jemima Howe, Mrs. Submit Grout, and Mrs. Eunice Gaffield.

Their husbands I need not mention again, and their feelings at this junction I will not attempt to describe. They had heard the enemies' guns. but knew not what had happened to their friends. Extremely anxious for their safety, they stood longing to embrace them, until at length, concluding from the noise thay heard without that some of them were come, they unbarred the gate in a hurry to receive them; when lo! to their inexpressible disappointment and surprise, instead of their husbands, in rushed a number of hideous Indians, to whom they and their tender offspring became an easy pray; and from whom they had nothing to expect but either an immediate death, or a long captivity. The latter of these, by favor of Providence, turned out to be the lot of these unhappy women, and their still more unhappy. because more helpless, children Mrs. Gaffield had but one, Mrs. Grout had three, and Mrs. Howe seven. The eldest of Mrs. Howe's was eleven years old, and the youngest but six months.

The two eldest were daughters, which she had by her first husband, Mr. William Phipps, who was also slain by the Indians, of which I doubt not but you have see an account in Mr. Doolittle's history. It was from the mouth of this woman that I lately received the foregoing account. She also gave me, I doubt not, a true, though, to be sure, a very brief and imperfect history of her captivity, which I here insert for your perusal. The Indians, (she says) having plundered and put fire to the fort, we marched, as near as I could judge, a mile and a half into the woods, where we encamped that night. When the morning came, and we had advanced as much farther, six Indians were sent back to the place of our late abode, who collected a little more plunder, and destroyed some other effects that had been left behind ; but they did not return until the day was so far spent, that it was judged best to continue where we were through the night. Early the next morning we set off for Canada, and continued our march eight days successfully, until we had reached the place where the Indians had left their canoes, about fifteen miles from Crown Point. This was a long and tedious march ; but the captives, by divine assistance, were enabled to endure it with less trouble and difficulty than they had reason to expect.

From such savage masters, in such indignant circumstances, we could not rationally hope for kinder treatment than we received. Some of us it is true, had a harder lot than others; and among the children, I thought my son Squire had the hardest of any. He was then only four years old, and when we stopped to rest our weary limbs, and he sat down on his master's pack, the savage monster would often knock him off; and sometimes too with the handle of his hatchet. Several ugly marks, indented in his head by the cruel Indians, at that tender age, are still plainly to be seen. At length we arrived at Crown Point, and took up our quarters there, for the space of near a week. In the meantime, some of the Indians went to Montreal, and took several of the weary captives along with them, with a view of selling them to the French. They did not succeed however, in finding a market for any of them. They gave my youngest daughter to the governor, de Vaudreuil, had a drunken frolic, and returned again to Crown Point, with the rest of their prisoners. From hence we set off for St. John's, in four or five canoes, just as night was coming on, and were soon surrounded with darkness. A heavy storm hung over us. The sound of the rolling thunder was very terrible upon the waters, which at every flash of expansive lightning seemed to be all in a blaze. Yet to this we were indebted for all the light we enjoyed. No object could we discern any longer than the flashes lasted.

In this posture we sailed in our open tottering canoes, almost the whole of that dreary night. The morning indeed had not yet begun to dawn, when we all went ashore; and having collected a heap of sand gravel for a pillow, I laid myself down, with my tender infant by my side not knowing where any of my other children were or what a miserable condition they might be in. The next day, however, under the wing of that ever present and all powerful Providence, which had preserved us through the darkness and imminent dangers of the preceding night, we all arrived in safety at St. John's. Our next movement was to St. Francois, the metropolis, if I may call it, to which the Indians, who led us captive, belonged. Soon after our arrival at that wretched capital, a council, consisting of the chief Sachem, and some principal warriors of the St. Francois tribe, was convened; and after the ceremonies usual on such occasions were over, I was conducted and delivered to an old squaw, who the Indians told me I must call my mother. My infant still continued to be the property of its original Indian owners. I was nevertheless permitted to keep it with me a while longer, for the sake of saving them the trouble of looking after it. When the weather began to grow cold, shuddering at the prospect of approaching winter, I acquainted my new mother, that I did not think it would be possible for me to endure it, if I must spend it with her, and share as the Indians did.

Listening to my repeated and earnest solicitations that I might be disposed of among some of the French inhabitants of Canada, she at length set off with me and my infant, attended by some male Indians, upon a journey to Montreal, in hopes of finding a market for me there. But the attempt proved unsuccessful, and the journey tedious indeed.

Our provision was so scanty as well as insipid and unsavory; the weather was so cold, and the traveling so very bad, that it often seemed as if I must have perished on the way. While we were at Montreal, we went into the house of a certain French gentleman, whose lady being sent for, and coming into the room where I was, to examine me, seeing I had an infant, exclaimed with an oath, "I will not buy a woman who has a child to look after." There was a swill pail standing near me, in which I observed some crusts of bread swimming on the surface of the greasy liquor it contained. Sorely pinched with hunger, I skimmed them off with my hands, and ate them; and this was all the refreshment which the house afforded r e. Somewhere in the course of this visit to Montreal, my Indian mother was so unfortunate as to catch the smallpox, of which distemper she died, soon after our return, which was by water, to St. Francois. And now came on the season when the Indians began to prepare for a winter's hunt.

I was ordered to return my poor child to those of them who still claimed it as their property. This was a severe trial. The babe clung to my bosom with all its might; but I was obliged to pluck it thence, and deliver it, shrieking and screaming enough to penetrate a heart of stone, into the hands of those unfeeling wretches, whose tender mercies may be termed cruel. It was soon carried off by a hunting party of those Indians, to a place called Metliskow, at the lower end of

Lake Champlain, whither, in about a month after it was my fortune to follow them. And here I found it, it is true, but in a condition that afforded me no great satisfaction; it being greatly emaciated and almost starved. I took it in my arms, put its face to mine, and it instantly bit me with such violence, that it seemed as if I must have parted with a piece of my cheek. I was permitted to lodge with it that, and the two following nights; but every morning that intervened, the Indians, I suppose on purpose to torment me, sent me away to another wigwam, which stood at a little distance, though not so far from the one in which my distressed infant was confined, but that I could plainly hear its incessant cries, and heartrending lamentations. In this deplorable condition, I was obliged to take my leave of it, on the morning of the third day after my arrival at the place. We moved down the lake several miles the same day; and the night following was remarkable on account of the great earthquake which terribly shook that howling wilderness.

Among the islands hereabouts, we spent the winter season, often shifting our quarters, and roving about from one place to another; our family consisting of three persons only, beside myself, viz.: my late mother's daughter, whom therefore I called my sister, her sanhop, and a pappoose. They once left me alone two dismal nights; and when they returned to me again, perceiving them smile at each other, I asked what is the matter? They replied, that two of my children were no more. One of which, they said, died a natural death, and the other was knocked on the head. I did not utter many words, but my heart was sorely pained within me, and my mind exceedingly troubled with strange and awful ideas. I often imagined, for instance, that I plainly saw the naked carcasses of my deceased children hanging upon the limbs of the trees, as the Indians are wont to hang the raw hides of those beasts which they take in hunting. It was not long, however, before it was ordered by kind Providence, that I should be relieved in a good measure from those horrid imaginations; for as I was walking one day upon the ice, observing a smoke at some distance upon the land, it must proceed, thought I, from the fire of some Indian hut; and who knows but some one of my poor children may be there. My curiosity, thus excited, led me to the place, and there I found my son Caleb, a little boy between two and three years old, whom I had lately buried, in sentiment at least; or rather imagined to have been deprived of life, and perhaps also denied a decent grave.

I found him likewise in tolerable health and circumstances, under the protection of a fond Indian mother; and moreover had the happiness of lodging with him in my arms one joyful night. Again we shifted our quarters, when we had traveled eight or ten miles upon the snow and ice, came to a place where the Indians manufactured sugar which they extracted from maple trees. Here an Indian came to visit us, whom I knew, and who could speak English. He asked me why I did not go to see my son Squire. I replied that I had lately been informed that he was dead. He assured me that he was yet alive, and but two or three miles off, on the opposite side of the Lake. At my request, he gave me the best directions he could to the place of his abode. I resolved to embrace the first opportunity that offered of endeavoring to search it out. While I was busy in contemplating this affair, the Indians obtained a little bread, of which they gave me a small share. I did not taste a morsel of it myself, but saved it all for my poor child, if I should be so lucky as to find him. At length, having obtained of my keepers leave to be absent for one day, I set off early in the morning, and steering, as well as I could, according to the directions which the friendly Indian had given me, I quickly found the place, which he had so accurately marked out.

I beheld, as I drew nigh, my little son without the camp; but he looked, thought I, like a starved and mangy puppy, that had been wallowing in the ashes. I took him in my arms, and he spoke to me these words, in the Indian tongue: "Mother, are you come?" I took him into the wigwam with me, and observing a number of Indian children in it, I distributed all the bread which I had reserved for my own child, among them all: otherwise I should have given great offence. My little boy appeared to be very fond of his new mother, kept as near me as possible while I stayed; and when I told him I must go, he fell as though he had been knocked down with a club. But having recommended him to the care of Him who made him, when the day was far spent, and the time would permit me to stay no longer, I departed, you may well suppose, with a heavy load at my heart. The tidings I had received of the death of my youngest child had, a little before, been confirmed to me beyond a doubt; but I could not mourn so heartily for the deceased, as for the living child.

When the winter broke up, we removed to St. John's; and through the ensuing summer, our principal residence was at no great distance from the fort at that place. In the meantime, however, my sister's husband having been out with a scouting party to some of the English settlements, had a drunken frolic at the fort, when he returned. His wife, who never got drunk, but had often experienced the ill effects of her husband's intemperance, fearing what the consequence might prove, if he should come home in a morose and turbulent humor, to avoid his insolence, proposed that we should both retire, and keep out of the reach of it, until the storm abated. We absconded accordingly ; but so it happened, that I returned, and ventured into his presence, before his wife had presumed to come nigh him. I found him in his wigwam, and in a surly mood ; and not being able to revenge upon his wife, because she was not at home, he laid hold of me, and hurried me to the fort ; and for a trifling consideration, sold me to a French gentleman, whose name was Saccapee.

It is an ill wind certainly that blows nobody any good. I had been with the Indians a year lacking fourteen days ; and, if not for my sister, yet for me, it was a lucky circumstance indeed, which thus at last, in an unexpected moment, snatched me out of their cruel hands, and placed me beyond the reach of their insolent power. After my Indian master had disposed of me in the manner related above, and the moment of sober reflection had arrived, perceiving that the man who had bought me had taken the advantage of him in an unguarded hour, his resentment began to kindle, and his indignation rose so high, that he threatened to kill me if he should meet me alone ; or if he could not revenge himself thus, that he would set fire to the fort. I was therefore secreted in an upper chamber, and the fort carefully guarded, until his wrath had time to cool. My service in the family to which I was advanced, was perfect freedom, in comparison with what it had been among the barbarous Indians.

My new master and mistress were both as kind and generous towards me as I could reasonably expect. I seldom asked a favor of either of them, but it was readily granted. In consequence of which I had it in my power, in many instances, to administer aid and refreshment to the poor prisoners of my nation, who were brought into St. John's during my abode in the family of the above mentioned benevolent and hospitable Saccapee. Yet even in this family, such trials awaited me as

I had little reason to expect ; but stood in need of a large stock of prudence, to enable me to encounter them. In this I was greatly assisted by the governor, and Colonel Schuyler, who was then a prisoner. I was moreover under unspeakable obligations to the governor on another account. I had received intelligence from my daughter Mary, the purport of which was, that there was a prospect of her being shortly married to a young Indian of the tribe of St. Francois, with which tribe she had continued from the beginning of her captivity. These were heavy tidings, and added greatly to the poignancy of my other afflictions.

However, not long after I had heard this melancholy news, an opportunity presented of acquainting that humane and generous gentleman, the commander-in-chief, and my illustrious benefactor, with this affair also, who, in compassion for my sufferings, and to mitigate my sorrows, issued his orders in good time and had my daughter taken away from the Indians, and conveyed to the same nunnery where her sister was then lodged, with his express injunction, that they should both of them together be well looked after, and carefully educated, as his adopted children. In this school * * * * they continued while the war in those days between France and Great Britain lasted. At the conclusion of which war, the governor went went home to France, took my oldest daughter along with him, and married her there to a French gentleman, whose name is Cron Lewis.

He was at Boston with the fleet under Count de Estaing, (1778) and one of his clerks. My other daughter still continuing in the nunnery, a considerable time had elapsed after my return from captivity, when I made a journey to Canada, resolving to use my best endeavors not to return without her. I arrived just in time to prevent her being sent to France. She was to have gone in the next vessel that sailed for that place. And I found it extremely difficult to prevail with her to quit the nunnery and go home with me. Yea, she absolutely refused; and all the persuasions and arguments I could use with her were to no effect, until after I had been to the governor, and obtained a letter from him to the superintendent of the nuns, in which he threatened, if my daughter should not be delivered immediately into my hands, or could not be prevailed with to submit to my parental authority, that he would send a band of soldiers to assist me in bringing her away.

But so extremely bigoted was she to the customs and religion of the place, that after all, she left it with the greatest reluctance, and the most bitter lamentations, which she continued as we passed the streets, and wholly refused to be comforted. My good friend, Major Small, whom we met on the way, tried all he could to console her; and was so very kind and obliging as to bear us company, and carry my daughter behind him on horseback. But I have run on a little before my story; for I have not yet informed you of the means and manner of my own redemption; to the accomplishment of which, the recovery of my daughter, just mentioned, and the ransoming of some of my children, several gentlemen of note contributed not a little; to whose goodness, therefore I am greatly indebted, and sincerely hope I shall never be so ungrateful as to forget it.

Colonel Schuyler, in particular, was so very kind and generous as to advance 2700 livres to procure a ransom for myself and three children. He accompanied and conducted us from Montreal to Albany, and entertained us in the most friendly and hospitable manner a considerable time at his own house, and I believe entirely at his own expense.

A Pioneer's Hardships.

Perhaps no better example of the hardships suffered by the early pioneers can be obtained than the recital of the experiences of Noadiah Hubbard, a man of rare individuality, pluck and natural ability. In 1853 he thus wrote of his early experiences:

I first came to this town, Champion, in the year 1797, with Lemuel Storrs, a large landholder, when he came on for the first time to view his purchase. I was then residing in Steuben, in what is now Oneida County, but then, or shortly before, Herkimer. Mr. Storrs then hired several pack men, whose business it was to carry the necessary provisions for the expedition on their backs. This was late in the autumn. We traveled on foot by what was called the French Road to the High Falls on the Black River. This road had been cut for the accommodation of the French refugees who had made a settlement at High Falls, and had then a log city. Many of these French belonged to the nobility of France, who were obliged to abandon their country during the revolution in 1793, but who were afterwards permitted to return when the star of empire rose upon the Bonapartes. Their settlement was made upon what was called the French Tract, on the north and east side of the Black River, and extending a great distance. From the High Falls we descended the river in a boat to the rapids, called Long Falls, now known as Carthage. Here we landed, and in two days explored the township, then an unbroken wilderness. On our way down, Silas Stow, then a young man, and afterward known as Judge Stow, of Lowville, joined us. On the third day we re-embarked and proceeded up the river, and it was two days hard rowing to get back again to High Falls. As I believe I before mentioned, it was late in November, and the night we were obliged to be out, we encountered a severe snow storm. To protect ourselves from it in some measure, we made a shanty by setting up some crotches, and laying on poles, and covering them with hemlock boughs. We also scattered branches upon the ground upon which to lie, and by making a rousing fire in front of our shelter, we contrived to be very comfortable. By this time our provisions were nearly exhausted, and we had before us the prospect of a hungry day. But in ascending the river we fortunately killed a duck and a partridge; these being stripped of their feathers in the evening, I cooked them for our breakfast the next morning. I prepared them as nicely as we could with our scanty means; salt we had none. I had a little pork left; this I cut in small bits and inserted into the flesh of the fowls, when it served the double purpose of salt, and butter for basting. To cook them I set up a couple of crotched sticks, laid another across, and from it by strips of bark suspended my fowls before the fire, where they cooked most beautifully, and were all in good time partaken of by the company with rare relish. Indeed, Messrs. Storrs and Stow declared they had never eaten so good. Hunger and a limited supply gave a keenness of relish not often experienced.

In due time we arrived safe and well in Steuben, from whence we had started, where I passed the winter. Mr. Storrs offered me very liberal inducements to come on here and accept them, though I may say in passing and then dismiss the subject forever, that he failed to fulfill his liberal offers. But in consideration of those offers, I left my home in Steuben the 1st of June, 1798, and started for this place, accompanied by Salmon Ward and David Starr, with fifteen head of cattle. We traveled again upon the French road, as far as it availed us. This township had been surveyed by Benjamin and Moses Wright, the year before, and this year Mr. Storrs had engaged B. W. to survey Hounsfield, and on his way there he was to mark a road to this place, and to precede me. I met the surveyors agreeably to appointment at a Mr. Hoadley's, and from there we came on to what is called Turin Four Corners. There was only one log house there then. From there we went west about thirty or forty rods to Zaccheus Higby's. There we laid down our maps and consulted them, and came to the conclusion to take from thence a north course. This led us upon to the top of a hill, now known as the Tug Hill. We were entirely ignorant of the face of the country, and of the most eligible route to pursue, and therefore took the one which seemed the most direct, not knowing the obstacles to be encountered. We had before come down by water, and on this route there was not even a marked tree. It was the duty of the surveyors to precede us, mark a road and chain it. Mr. W. started in advance of us for this purpose. It was a beautiful, clear morning and we followed on, progressing finely until the middle of the afternoon, when we came to a gulf, and an abundance of marked trees. We went over the gulf but could find no more trees marked. We then made a fire and took out the stoppings from our bells, and suffered

A PIONEER'S HARDSHIPS.

our cattle to feed around the fire, while we set ourselves to search for marked trees, over the gulfs and up and down, but could find no place to cross, or marks by which to determine what course the surveyors had taken. In this predicament we prepared to construct a shelter for the night of hemlock boughs.

The next morning the sun came up clear and bright, and I called a council. I told the men how much damage it would be to me to return, how great a loss not to proceed, and asked them if they were willing to come on. David Starr replied that he would go to h—l, if I would. Though no way desirous of going to the latter place, even in good company, I determined to come on, if such a thing were possible, without a compass or guide. We then set ourselves to work, and felled trees, with which we made an enclosure, into which we drove our cattle, and then shoved them down the precipice, one after another; they went up slantingly on the other side, and much better than we got them down, so that finally they were all safely over, after much toil and trouble. I then agreed to pilot the company down, took off the ox bell; and carried it in my hand, leading the way, and steered a north course by the sun and watch. We had the advantage of a bright sunshine. We had to cross a number of gulfs, and one windfall, which was the worst of all. We continued to travel upon the summit of the hill, where we found much fine table land. The cattle would travel as fast as I could lead the way. One man drove them, and another followed, axe in hand, to mark the trees, and leave traces behind us, so that if we could not advance, we could trace our steps.

We descended the hill before reaching Deer River. The latter we struck and crossed above the falls—not far from where the village of Copenhagen now stands—and coming on, we succeeded in finding the town line, which was identified by marked trees, not far from where the toll-gate now is, on the Champion and Copenhagen Plank Road. We then changed our course, following the line to the Black River, at Long Falls, where we arrived before night. We there found Mr. W. and men. They had not arrived more than an hour before us. When seeing us, Mr. W. exclaimed:

"How, in the name of God, have you got here?" I replied:

"You scoundrel! you ought to be burnt for leaving us so!"

It was a most rascally piece of business, their leaving us as they did. But I suppose the truth was, they thought it impossible for us ever to get through with our cattle; but this does not excuse them for not having marked the road; 'twas for that they were sent—and if others could not follow, they were not answerable; but their duty was plain before them.

My boat, which I had dispatched from the High Falls, soon after arrived, with my provisions, yokes, chains, and cooking utensils. The next day we left one to watch our effects, while the others were searching for a desirable location. In a few days I selected the farm upon which I now live, principally for the reason that it was the centre of the township, rather than for any peculiar advantages it possessed over other portions of the town. Yet the soil has proved good, and sufficiently luxuriant with proper cultivation. This was what I sought, a good agricultural location, rather than one possessing hydraulic privileges.

Not one tree had been cut here for the purpose of making a settlement, nor was there a white man settled in what is now the county of Jefferson, when I came here. I was the first white settler in the county. I remained here through the summer, and until October, engaged in making a clearing. We then returned to Steuben, where my family was, to spend the winter.

During the summer, some families had come into Lowville, and Mr. Storrs had caused a road to be marked from there to the Long Falls, and by that we returned, driving our cattle home again. These had become fat, by running in the woods, during the summer, and I sold them for beef. I would mention here, though rather out of place, that I found a living spring of pure water, a few rods before where the public house, in Champion, now stands, which had its influence in deciding my location. Near it I built my first house, and there I kept "bachelor's hall" two summers, being myself "chief cook." My first habitation was a cabin, erected in a few hours' time, with the aid of my men. It was a rude structure, but served our purpose. We first set some posts, and then, having felled great trees, stripped them of the bark, and, with this, covered the roof and three sides of our dwelling, the front was left opened, so that it may truly be said, we kept open house. The covering was kept firmly in its place by withes of bark. After the completion of our house, the next most necessary thing, was an oven, in which to bake our bread, for bread we must have, it being the staff of life. This was soon made, with two logs for a foundation, and a flat stone thereon, the superstructure was soon reared with smaller stones, cemented together by a mortar of muck, from the side of the spring, and crowned by a flat stone. This answered my purpose as well as one of more elaborate construction. For a door, we split out a plank of basswood; and for a kneading-trough, we again had recourse to the basswood, from whence we cut a log of the required length and dimensions, split it, and from one half, dug out, with an axe, and an instrument named a howell, which we had brought for such purposes, in a short time, a trough, which answered our purpose very well. I brought some yeast with me, to make my first batch of bread; after that, I used leaven, kept and prepared after directions given me by my wife, before leaving home. Whatever may be said of our cooking, in general, I am sure none ever seemed sweeter to me, or was eaten with a better relish by others: labor sweetened every mouthful. We had cows and plenty of milk. We sometimes washed dishes, when we could not remember what we last ate upon them, but oftener turned them the bottom side up, there to remain until wanted again. Some even pretend to say, that when our table needed scouring, we sprinkled salt upon it, and put it out for the old cow to operate upon. However that may be, I am sure, if we ever did do it, it must have come from under her scouring apparatus exceedingly white. But the whole story is rather aprocryphal.

Early in the spring, 1799, I sent on two men, to make sugar, before I came on myself. They commenced making sugar, and one day went out hunting, leaving their sugar boiling. The consequence was, the house took fire and burned down, with all of the little it contained. During the winter, the Indians had stolen all the cooking utensils I had left, and the potatoes which I had raised, and buried the autumn before. Thus my riches were taking to themselves wings, and flying away. I came on soon after. This spring, Esquire Mix and family came on; John and Thomas Ward, Ephraim Chamberlain, Samuel and David Starr, Jotham Mitchell, Salmon Ward and Bela Hubbard, David Miller, and Boutin, a Frenchman, came to Carthage. The above were all young, unmarried men, save Mix. We continued our labors through the summer of 1799, but not with that spirit which we should have done, had not a rumor reached us of the failure of Mr.

Storrs, and the probability that we should lose, not only all our labor, but the money which I had advanced for my land. But I will not enter into particulars here—let it suffice that I could not afford to lose all I had done and paid, and consequently entered into a compromise with him, to save a moiety of what was justly mine—of not only what I had actually paid for, but of what I was to have had, for leading the way in this first settlement of a new country, and subjecting myself again to all its discomforts and inconveniences. Consequently, in view of making this my permanent home, I moved my family here in the autumn of 1799. We had a very unfavorable time, to come. There had been a snow storm, in which about six inches of snow had fallen. We were obliged to travel on horseback, the horses' feet balled badly; we had sloughs to go through, and altogether, it was very uncomfortable traveling in that manner, with children. We arrived at Mr. Hoadley's the first night, and our ox-teams and goods the next day. From there, we came to the High Falls, where I had a boat awaiting us, which I had caused to be built for my own use. Here we embarked with all our goods and chattels, of all kinds, loading the boat to its utmost capacity, so that when all were in, it was only about four inches out of water.

We spent one night at the Lowville landing, where a family were living. During the evening, there came in a number of men, wet, cold and hungry. Among them, was one named Smith. He went to pull off the boots of one of his companions, which was very wet and clinging close. He pulled with all his might—the other bracing himself against him as firmly as possible. All at once, and with unexpected suddeness, the boot came off, and poor Smith was sent with his bare feet, into a bed of live coals. There was both music and dancing for one while.

We arrived at the Long Falls, about noon, the second day from our embarkation. The weather had by this time become warm and pleasant. Our oxen arrived soon after by land, we unloaded our boat, put our wagon together, loaded it with some of our effects, set off, and, before night, reached our "wilderness home.' My wife said in view of the difficulties in getting here, that if she had anything as good as a cave to live in, she would not return in one year at least. She, of choice, walked from the Falls here, a distance of four miles through the forest. We arrived on the 17th of Nov., 1799. The weather continued pleasant until the 27th, when it commenced snowing, the river soon froze over, the snow, of which a great quantity fell, and continuing to fall, lasted all winter, and we were entirely cut off from all intercourse with the world. I kept fifteen head of cattle through the winter, by browsing them, and they wintered well. Isolated though we were, yet I never passed a more comfortable winter. We had a plenty of provisions; my wheat, I had raised here, a very fine crop from seed sown in the autumn of 1798, and my pork, etc., was fattened in Oneida County, and brought here by boat. And take it altogether, I perhaps settled this country as easy as any one ever settled a new country, as completely isolated as this was at that time, and easier than I settled in Steuben, 18 miles from Utica. At that time we had to go to Utica or Whitesborough for provisions, and it always took one day to go out, and another to return, incredible as it may now seem. In the spring of 1800, people began to flock into the country by hundreds, and, as my log house afforded the only accommodation for wayfaring men, we were obliged to keep them, whether we would or no; sometimes, and that very often, my floors were strewn with human beings as thick as they could lie, some so near the huge fire place as not to pass unscorched;

one man in particular, it was said by his companions, had his head baked, by too close a proximity to the oven. This rush continued two or three years, and was full of incident and interest, but at this distance of time I can not recall these incidents with sufficient accuracy to detail them here. The town settled rapidly with an intelligent and energetic class of people. The society was good ; it might be called good any where. Perhaps there was never a more intelligent and interesting people congregated together in an obscure little inland town, than in this, within a few years from its first settlement. I can not state the order of time in which they came, but the names of a few of them I will record, that in future time, when this place shall have sunk into insignificance, as it too probably will, before the greater lights arising around it, it may be known that we were once honored by having in our midst such men as Egbert Ten Eyck, afterwards first judge of the court, who was then a young lawyer, and married here, to one of our beautiful maidens ; Olney Pearce and wife, Hubbel and wife, Judge Moss Kent, brother of the late chancellor, Henry R. Storrs, who opened an office here, and afterwards became one of the most distinguished lawyers of the state. Dr. Baudry, a Frenchman, Drs. Durkee and Farley, and many others, too numerous to mention, as well as many ladies of grace and beauty, whom it would be invidious now to particularize. Common schools were soon established. Religious meetings were held on the Sabbath, after old Deacon Carter came into the town, and in a very few years, I think as early as 1805, the Rev. Nathaniel Dutton came. He was sent out by some missionary society at the east, to form churches in this western world, and coming to this place, was invited to remain, which he did, and continued here until the close of his valuable life, in Sept. 1852, and for the greater part of that time was the pastor of the Congregational church, which flourished under his ministrations, and enjoyed many powerful revivals of religion.

Folk-Stories.

The following stories, some of them worn threadbare in a past generation will come back to older readers like the sweet voice of a bird in the desert. What memories the almost-forgotten anecdote revives! Golden vision of days when the heart was young, and sympathy, pure, deep and tearful ruled the soul. A sympathy that wept with the new homesick puppy; released the imprisoned mother hen fussing in her coop, or removed the pebble from a struggling shoot. The simple, unselfish mind of a child that makes a confident of the domestic animals, and gives the creeping vine a helping hand to a new or firmer hold. A sympathy alas! all too soon hardened by experience and self interests.

Every person had, as a child, his or her favorite story told over and again, and at each repetition a new scene was mirrored upon the curtain of childish imagination. The good old story of how a chief tested the confidence of a leading colonist has gotten into print and is thus delightfully related in Pansy, though differing slightly in detail.

HAN YERRY.

Old Han Yerry, was an Indian chief of the Oneida tribe, who lived in the northern part of New York State a hundred years ago. He had fought with the king's party against the colonists; but, after the war, when Judge White came to found the town of Whitesborough, he sought to make friends with them. The judge was the first white man to form a settlement there. He was surrounded by Indians, but was kind and good, and soon won their love. He lived in a small log house, with his married daughter and a little grandchild, who was about two or three years old.

One day, old Han Yerry, with his squaw and a mulatto servant, came from Oriskany, three miles away, to pay the judge a visit and renew their friendship. Before going, the chief said:

"I like you and have confidence in you. Do you like me and have you confidence in me?" To which the judge replied warmly that he liked him and had confidence in him.

"Then prove it to me," said the old chief. "My squaw loves your papoose. Let us take her back to remain all night. I will return with her in the morning."

The baby's poor mother sat speechless with terror at the thought of trusting her darling to these savages, and, as she saw signs of yielding in her father's face, threw herself distractedly at his feet. Without looking at her distress, he gently took the child from her close embrace, and told her she had nothing to fear from their good friends, who would surely bring her back safely and well. Then, placing the child in the squaw's arms, he said: "I trust to my friends all that I hold most dear."

Though he looked calm and smiling, he deeply felt the sacrifice he was called upon to make in order to save the colonists, who would have perished had the request been refused.

All night they kept vigil, and in the first gray light of

dawn strained their eyes up the road for sign of any human being; but there was none. The hours came and went—noon, afternoon. Still no sign. In silence and prayer, with dark foreboding, they kept watch. Sometimes the poor mother, through grief and fear, would try to rush up the road in search of her darling, but was restrained by her father, who knew that such a breach of confidence would cause its death and that of the defenseless settlers, while reliance on their word would increase friendliness. So, hand in hand, they waited.

At last, as the sun sank behind the hills, some figures appeared in the distance. Almost breathlessly they observed them approach. As they drew nearer, with a cry of delight, the keen eyes of the mother saw Blossom perched on the shoulders of the old chief, dressed out in all the gorgeousness of an Indian princess, instead of her own little clothes, smiling and happy, as if she had had the best of times, as indeed was the case; for the Indians had been very kind and tender in their efforts to amuse the little " Pale Flower."

Judge White was wise to show the Indians this great trust, for they never forgot it. From that time they did all they could to aid the white settlers at Sedaghquate, afterward called Whitesborough, and to show their love and respect for them.

A COURT OF RECORD.

An act was passed, April, 1806, directing three terms of the court of common pleas to be held in Jefferson and Lewis counties. Tradition says, that, after formal adjournment, the first court, which was held in the school house, on the ground now covered by the Universalist Church, became a scene of fun and frolic, which has since been seldom equaled. The greater part of the settlers were young or middle aged men, some indulged in habits of intemperance; the custom of the day did not discountenance practical joking, and athletic games were invariably the accompaniment of all gatherings. Moreover they had been just organized, and must have business for their courts, else what the need of having courts? Should any one evince a disinclination to join in these proceedings, they were accused of "sneakism," and arraigned before a mock tribunal, where, guilty or not guilty, the penalty of a "quarter," was sure to be imposed for the benefit of the crowd. Among other charges was one against Esq. H., of Rutland, a man of very sober and candid character, who was charged with stealing. Conscious of innocence, he offered to be searched, when a quantity of dough was found in both pockets of his coat. Thus implicated by circumstances which he could not explain, he was fined. Another was accused of falling asleep, and fined a shilling, and another was fined a like sum for smoking in the court room. After paying the penalty, he resumed his pipe, and was again arraigned, when he entered his plea that the fine was for a pipe full, which he had not finished, and this afforded a subject of legal argument for discussion, that elicited the research and ability of the lawyers present. As the avowed intention was to make business for all the new officers, one was stripped and laid out on a board, loosely covered with a cloth, and a coroner sent for, who commenced a bona fide examination, that was interrupted by some one tipping over the board, when the "subject" of the hoax jumped up and fled. There had not thus far been any business for the sheriff, but this was at length made, by their finding one who had crept into the garret for concealment. He was dragged before their tribunal, where it was decided that his failing was a disease, rather than a crime, and required a specific. This carnival was continued the second day, and although the officers of the court affected to abstain from these frolics, yet judicial dignity offered no exemption from them, and all parties, whether willing or unwilling, were compelled to join. Companies, distinguished by personal peculiarities, were paraded under officers selected for the prominence of these traits, as "long noses," etc., while the little short men were organized into a party and charged with the duty of "keeping the cats off." These follies may be considered puerile, but not more so than the annual carnival in some European countries, and their record is interesting from illustrating the custom of the times, when athletic games were fashionable, and men seldom met in numbers without having "a regular train."

A MIGHTY NIMROD.

The following encounter with a panther, in 1819, was related by Jairus Rich, the hunter: It occurred near Hyde Lake, about three miles from the village of Plessis. He had set his traps for wolves, and had arrived within a few rods of one of them, when he observed a panther spring up and run with a trap to one of his hind legs. He fired, but missed the mark, and his game made off into the thicket, when he returned to a house nearly a mile distant, procured a small dog, and having again repaired to the place, and stationed himself where he could start the entrapped animal, he observed the head of a panther emerge from the bushes about five rods distant, upon which he fired and killed him instantly. He soon found that this was not the one in the trap, and a heavy shower of rain coming on, he found it difficult to load his rifle again, which he at length did. The dog, meanwhile, had engaged the other panther, upon which he fired and wounded him, and finding he could not reload, on account of the rain, he threw down his piece, and seizing his hatchet, sprung upon him, when there ensued a fearful struggle, in which, finally, the beast got under, with one of the man's hands in his mouth ; the hatchet was lost, but with the other hand he drew from his pocket a knife, opened it with his teeth, and finally succeeded in cutting the throat of the ferocious animal. The hunter was badly torn, but made out to crawl to the nearest house, where, after many weeks, he recovered, but carried the scars of the conflict with him to the grave. The bounties for the destruction of wild animals were then so great, that the inducements for gain led to ingenious measures for securing the rewards, and it is related of the same person, that having trailed a she wolf to her den, and killed her, he found in the cave ten young whelps, but too small to be entitled to the bounty. He accordingly built a pen in the forest, and fed them daily upon wild meats which he obtained in hunting, until they were grown. He became strongly attached to one of them, who would follow him like a dog, but the temptation of $50 was too strong to resist, and he slew his favorite pet to gain the premium. This breeding wolves for the market, had its parallel in an instance in this town, in which a hunter, to gain the reward that might be offered for the secret, professed to know of a salt spring, to which he was induced to conduct a certain person, and in which he had a little previous buried a bag of salt. The water being duly "analyzed," by measuring, evaporating, and weighing, a purchase of nearly 800 acres was made, without a knowledge of the spring by the landholder, nor was the trick discovered before the bargain had been sealed and the sale perfected.

A SURVEYING INCIDENT.

Charles C. Brodhead, a native of Pennsylvania, had held the rank of captain in the Revolution, and while performing a survey, encountered many hardships. An obituary notice published soon after his death, which occurred in 1853, at Utica, contained the following:

"In running the great lines of division his party had crossed the Black River several times, the men and instruments being ferried across. On one occasion when they had approached the river, having journeyed through the woods without noting their route by the compass, they arrived at a part of the bank which they recognized, and knew to be a safe place of passing. Making a raft of logs, they started from the bank, and began to pole across. When in the midst of the current their poles failed to reach the bottom, and simultaneous with this discovery, the noise of the waters below them revealed the horrid fact that they had mistaken their ferrying place, and were at the head and rapidly approaching the Great Falls of the river, the passage of which threatened all but certain death. Instantly Mr. B. ordered every man who could swim to make for the shore, and he prepared to swim for his own life. But the piteous appeals of Mr. Pharoux, a young Frenchman of the party, who could not swim, arrested him, and he determined to remain with him to assist him, if possible, in the awful passage of the falls. Hastily directing his men to grasp firmly to the logs of the raft, giving similar directions to Mr. Pharoux, he then laid himself down by the side of his friend. The raft passed the dreadful falls and was dashed to pieces. Mr. Pharoux with several of the whites and Indians was drowned, and Mr. Brodhead himself thrown into an eddy near the shore, whence he was drawn almost senseless by an Indian of the party." The body of Pharoux afterwards was found on a small island at the mouth of the river to which his name was given. Mr. LeRay caused to be prepared a marble tablet to be inserted in the rocks here, with the following inscription:

"To the memory of Peter Pharoux, this Island is consecrated."

A MAN-TRAP—SMUGGLING.

In 1808, a party of militia, under Captain Timothy Tamblin, was stationed near the intersection of the two great roads leading into St. Lawrence County, a mile north of the village of Antwerp, to prevent smuggling under the embargo law. There was much opposition both in theory and practice to this law. An instance is related in which a practical joke of a somewhat serious nature, was played off upon one of these guardians of the national wellfare. A person to whom the law was odious, having set a trap in his sleigh, and placed around it a loading calculated to convey the impression that they were smuggled goods approached the guard, but warned those on duty to keep away from his load, or they would get into trouble. Not deterred by this threat, one of the guard proceeded rudely to overhaul the sleigh, to ascertain its contents, and was soon convinced that it at least concealed a trap, for it sprung upon his hand, at which the driver gave reins to his team and drove off exclaiming:

"I've caught a Democrat!"

During the war, a company of regular troops was stationed a little north of Antwerp village, to prevent smuggling into the country from Canada. The inducements which led to this were so strong, that much ingenuity was exercised in evading the vigilance of sentinels, and sometimes with great success. Five or six sleigh loads of tea had on a certain occasion been got to within three or four miles of Antwerp, having passed thus far without suspicion as the tea was packed in bags, like grain on its way to market. To evade the military guard that obstructed the road, the following stratagem was adopted: Captain B. who had charge of the company, was invited to a whist party at Cook's tavern, three miles north of Antwerp, at which place, during the evening, a large party of boys and young men assembled, with no apparent object but to spend the evening in carousing, drinking and card playing. Brandy circulated freely, and the revels continued till a late hour in the night, when the captain and his party set out to return in a sleigh closely followed by the loads of tea, thickly covered by a disorderly crowd, who by singing, shouting quarreling, and fighting, made the night hideous with unearthly discords, and would readily pass as a half drunken rabble returning from a midnight revel. The captain, who was himself rather more than half intoxicated, entered with spirit into the merriment of the others, and as the train approached the sentinels, he shouted:

"It's Captain B., let my company pass."

The order was obeyed, and the disorderly mob passed on, and having got beyond reach of danger, they left the teams to pursue their course in quiet, and in due time boasted of the success of their stratagem.

CORRUPT POLITICIANS.

At the annual town meeting in 1820, which was held at Perch River, after electing a portion of the officers, the meeting adjourned to the house of Edward Arnold, on Penet Square, until the next day. This measure created much excitement, and those living in the southern and eastern portions of the town, rallied with all their forces, attended promptly at the earliest moment of the adjourned meeting, organized, and immediately voted another adjournment to the house of Elias Bennet at Brownville village, on the afternoon of the same day, where the vote for town clerk was reconsidered, and the remaining officers elected. Being thus robbed of their town meeting, the settlers on Penet's Square and in distant localities, demanded a separate organization, which was readily consented to, and all parties having met at an informal meeting, or convention, at the village, agreed upon a petition to the legislature, which was acted upon, before another town meeting. The foregoing is a concise statement of the act of "stealing a town meeting," which gave rise to much talk at the time, and about which many fabulous stories have been related. It is said that this heinous crime of robbery was made the subject of a painting, that formed a part of a traveling exhibition.

GENERAL JACOB BROWN.

Brownville was first explored, with a view of settlement, by General Jacob Brown, who while teaching school in New York, had met with Rodolph Tillier, the general agent for the Chassanis lands, and was induced to purchase a large tract, and become the agent for commencing a settlement, at a time when the difficulties attending such an enterprise were very great. Having engaged in this business, he repaired in February, 1799, to the location of the French company, at the High Falls, and made several journeys to Utica, when, having completed his arrangements, and collected provisions at the Long Falls, he in March, 1799, passed down the old French road, in company with three or four hired men, and happening to reach the river at the mouth of Philomel Creek, he was charmed with the prospect of a water power, apparently perennial, and at once decided upon stopping here. He commenced clearing land, having sent for his father's family, who started on the 22d of April, from Bucks County, Pa., and after stopping a few days at New York and Schenectady, and hiring at Utica an extra boat, at length arrived at the location on the 17th of May, 1799, having been nearly three weeks on the road. George Brown, a relative, came on in the same company, with a part of his family, making, with the boatman, a party of nearly twenty. The boatman soon returned, leaving one boat that served the means for communication with Kingston, from whence they derived most of their provisions, the stock left at the Long Falls having been sold. When this company had arrived, the first had cleared a small piece, and got up the body of a log house, twenty feet square, which occupied the site of the hay scales on the edge of the bank, in the village, and the same season they put up the body of a two-story log house, 25 by 30, on the ground covered by the store of Wm. Lord. This was not, however, completed for occupation till the spring of 1801. In the fall of 1800 a saw mill was built at the mouth of Philomel Creek, the millwrights being Noah Durrin and Ebenezer Hills, and late in the fall of 1801 a grist mill was built for Mr. Brown, by Ethni Evans, afterwards the pioneer of Evans Mills. A few goods were brought on with the first family, but in the fall of the same year, Jacob Brown went to New York, on other business, and selected a small stock better adapted to the market. In 1799, a great number came in to look for lands, many of whom selected farms on Perch river, and between that place and Brownville, where they commenced small clearings, and made arrangements for removal with their families in the spring.

In 1804, the question of forming one or more new counties from Oneida, became the absorbing theme,and a convention was held at Denmark, Nov. 20, 1804, to decide upon the application, at which most of the delegates are said to have gone prepared to vote for one county, but from the influence of Mr. Brown, and Gen. Martin, of Martinsburg, were induced to apply for the erection of two new counties. In locating the county seat, the most active efforts were made in each county, Martinsburgh and Lowville being the rivals in Lewis, and Watertown and Brownville in Jefferson. Mr. Brown was the principal advocate of the latter, but the mass of settlement was then in the southern towns, and the portion north of Black River was known to be low, level, and (in a state of nature) much of it swampy. The settlements that had been begun at that early day, at Perch River, Chaumont, and on the St. Lawrence, were visited by severe sickness, and the idea was entertained, or at least held forth to the commissioners who located the site, that it could never be inhabited. Mr. Brown next endeavored to procure the location on the north bank of the river, near Watertown, and made liberal offers of land, for the public use, but the perseverance and intrigues of Mr. Coffeen and others, succeeded in fixing the site at its present location.

After the opening of the land office at Le Raysville, Mr. Brown continued for two or three years devoted to his private affairs, and meanwhile received unsolicited, commissions of captain, and of colonel of the 108th regiment of militia. His promotion in the line of military life, is said to have arisen from his avowed aversion to frequent and expensive military parades in time of peace, calling off the inhabitants from their labors in the fields, and encouraging habits of intemperance which in those days were too frequently the accompaniment of such gatherings. His views of the subject of militia organizations, approached more nearly to our present system; and in selecting him for office, the people were convinced, that while he omitted nothing conducive to the public safety, he would cause them no needless expense of time and money for parades. In his public and private conduct, and daily life, they saw him in possession of sagacity and intelligence, that led them to place confidence in his resources, should emergencies call for their exercise, and the integrity of his private life convinced them that the public trusts with which he might be honored, would be faithfully preserved.

In the discharge of his official duties, General Brown removed to Washington in 1821, where he continued to reside until his death, which occurred February 24, 1828, from the effect of a disease contracted at Fort Erie. For some time previous, his physical powers had been impaired by a paralytic stroke. His death was announced to the army by an order of the secretary of war; and the funeral ceremonies were performed with all the formality and dignity that his exalted rank required.

A BLOCKHOUSE GRANARY.

The inhabitants living on Perch River, on receiving the news of the war, were greatly alarmed from their supposed exposure on the frontier, and some of the timid ones resolved to leave the country. To dissuade them from this, it was proposed to build a blockhouse, which was forthwith done by voluntary labor, but when completed, only served as a storehouse for the wheat of a neighbor. Some, ridiculing the idea of danger, humorously proposed to post themselves on the brow of some of the limestone ledges towards Catfish Creek, in the direction of Canada, which would give them the double advantages of a commanding position, and an abundance of material for missiles, in case of attack. This had its effect, and after a few weeks' reflection the idea of Indian massacre was forgotten. It will be remembered that many of the older inhabitants had realized in their youth the horrors of Indian warfare and the tales of midnight massacre which they related as they assembled on evenings for mutual safety, enhanced, in no small degree, this timidity. Still the alarms which prevailed in this county were far less than those that spread through the St. Lawrence settlements, and as afterwards appeared in Canada itself, where nearly every family along the river had been fugitives from the desolating hand of war, from their adherence to the royal cause in the revolution. The apprehensions of both parties soon subsided, and men resumed their customary pursuits, except when occasional drafts or general alarms, called out the militia, or the emergencies of the service required the assembling of teams for the transportation of munitions of war. Prices of produce were, of course, extremely high, and from the large amount of government money expended here, the basis of many fortunes in the county were laid at that period.

BURIED TREASURE.

The aboriginal remains of Ellisburgh, have given occasion for the weak minded to believe that they were in some way concerned with buried treasures, and this being confirmed by the supposed indications of the divining rod, led in early times to explorations for them, despite of the guardianship of the spirits of the murdered, who according to the most approved demonologists of these speculations were in some instances charged with making money out of the credulous victims of superstition, by selling provisions, and in several instances, the diggers were almost frightened out of their senses by ghosts and demons; some got fleeced of substantial property in pursuit of imaginary wealth, and others lost the respect of sensible men by the favor with which they regarded these follies. On a certain occasion in preparing the enchanted circle for digging, a lamb was sacrificed to appease the guardian demons of the supposed treasure, but this act was generally regarded as a sacrilege and did much towards bringing discredit upon these heathenish orgies.

CUSTOMS TROUBLES.

In September, 1808, an event occurred in Ellisburgh that created great excitement at the time. A party from Oswego, under Lieut. Asa Wells, entered Sandy Creek, and after seizing a quantity of potash under the embargo laws, proceeded to the house of Capt. Fairfield, surrounded it, and seized and carried away a swivel. Mr. F. being absent, his wife made complaint to a justice, who issued a warrant. The constable was intimidated and called upon his fellow citizens to aid him, when about thirty men took arms and went with him, but Wells' men presented bayonets, when they desisted, and twenty of the men went off. Lieut. Wells ordered the remainder to be disarmed and bound, when they were taken with the swivel to Oswego. On the evening of the 25th of September, the same party returned, as reported, for the purpose of taking the magistrate and constable who had issued the papers. A warrant against Wells and two others for telony, in breaking open a house was issued at Sackets Harbor and given to Andrew Pease, a constable, to execute, who, after examining the law, raised a hue and cry and assembled about 200 persons in Ellisburgh, where a consultation of several magistrates was held, and the next day at sunrise about seventy or eighty men, armed and equipped, volunteered to aid in the arrest, but the magistrates durst not issue the order for their march, being apprehensive that some excess or injury might be done, and the question having been raised whether a constable had a right to demand aid, before he had been resisted, the armed men were advised to disperse, and the civil officer requested to proceed to apprehend Wells and the others, without the force of the county. This proceeding was charged by one of the political parties as an attempt of the other to resist by force of arms the execution of the laws, and mutual criminations were exchanged with much bitterness.

PETER PENET.

A tract of land, square in form, with the sides running coincident with the principal cardinal points, and its northwest corner resting upon the St. Lawrence at the mouth of French Creek, is "Penet's Square."

The revolution attracted to America many French adventurers, says Hough, some of whom had much more to gain than to lose, and among these was one Peter Penet, of Nantes, France. He arrived at Providence, R. I., by way of Cape Francois, (W. I.,) in December, 1775, having letters and credentials which at first secured him some attentions, and he obtained from a committee of congress a contract in the name of De Plaine, Penet & Co., for supplying a large amount of arms from France. He also made separate propositions to several of the colonies for powder, arms and ordnance, in the execution of which he proposed to ship a large amount of tobacco and other produce directly to France. He had various other speculations, all of which proved visionary, and it soon appeared that he was only a needy adventurer without capital or character. He succeeded in procuring advances, which were not accounted for, and he may be justly called "The Confidence Man" of the revolution. After the war he became an Indian trader and acquired a great ascendency among the Oneidas. When these people were holding a treaty with the state in 1788 for the cession of their lands, it was found expedient to consult with him and to ask his aid in promoting these measures; and as they were stipulating the reservations to be made for themselves and friends, he "dreamed" that they would give him a tract of land that he should locate somewhere north of Oneida Lake. His dream was fulfilled in the gift of ten miles square, which bears his name, but before the grant was perfected he fled from the country and the title passed to a creditor for a consideration of five shillings.

While operating upon the credulity of these simple people, he devised a plan of government for the Oneidas, that was to lead them to that perfection to which few civilized communities attain. The national affairs were to be managed by a Grand Council; all differences were to be settled by persons eminently wise and just; a tract of land was to be rented, and the revenues were to pay all public charges, of whatever amount; no lands were ever to be alienated, and no cause of complaint was ever to arise. It was resolved, as the highest incentive to virtue, "that as soon as convenient material can be procured, eighteen proper marks of distinction shall be given; three representing the tribe of the Bear; three the tribe of the Wolf; and three the tribe of the Tortoise.

The marks of the chiefs of war was a green ribbon striped on the side with red, to be worn on the left side. Nine marks of distinction for the chiefs of the coucillors, with the mark of an Eagle on a red ribbon, to go round the neck and hang between the breasts. Be it remembered that those chiefs, whether warriors or councillors, who wear this badge, must be men of truth, honor and wisdom to discharge the great trust of national business now put in their hands, and whether at home or abroad, when these marks are seen, it will be remembered that they are this great council and great respect will at all times be shown them."

This scheme of government, comprising twenty articles, contemplated the appointment of Peter Penet, their "true and trusted friend, adopted and chosen agent forever," as their principal executive agent, and being duly signed by marks (not one being able to read,) this state paper was published with great formality in the Albany newspapers. It is needless to add that it had not so much as a beginning of actual realization.

Some time after Penet had absconded, he made his appearance in San Domingo; at the time of the negro insurrection there, he invited his countrymen to buy lands on his estates in Northern New York. He exhibited a map with fortified cities, on the north shore of Oneida Lake, and by false representations, induced some to purchase lands. One of these unfortunates, upon arriving in New York, and learning how cruelly he had been deceived, was unable to bear up under the affliction, and died by his own hand. It is from Penet that this place on the St. Lawrence derived the name of "French Creek."

The successors to his title selected the mile-square nearest the river, as the site for a town, and caused it to be surveyed into ten-acre squares, except the quarter of a mile directly upon the river, in which each of these lots were further sub-divided into four. It was afterwards laid out as the village of "Cornelia," (named from Madame Jubel,) but since the organization of the town of Clayton, in 1833, it has borne this name.

In early times "French Creek" was a noted point for smuggling ; and especially in the embargo of 1807-8, when almost all of the region north of Black River was a forest, it became a principal point for importing goods, and for sending potash out of the country. It was found impossible to guard this frontier so as to prevent crossing with teams on the ice in winter, or by boats in summer, and the most that the authorities attempted, was to guard the roads in the interior, and intercept such contraband goods as they could discover.

A STEAMER BURNED.

The most disastrous accident that ever occurred on Lake Ontario happened near the Ducks, small islands near the Canadian shore, about forty miles from Kingston, on the morning of April 30, 1853. The upper cabin steamer Ocean Wave, built in Montreal, in 1851, and owned by the Northern Railroad, being then on her way down from Hamilton to Ogdensburgh, took fire between one and two o'clock in the morning, and was burned. The fire took near the engine, and appeared to have been occasioned by the faulty construction of the boat, which had been on fire on one or two previous occasions. When the flames were discoved they were making such rapid progress, from the boat being newly painted, that the small boats could not be got out, and in less than five minutes it was enveloped in flames. The terrific scene that ensued defies description, the miserable victims having but a moment's time for deciding by which mode of death they should perish. The light attracted the schooners Georgiana and Emblem, who, with some fishing boats from the shore, saved twenty-one persons out of forty-four, the number of the crew and passengers. The steamer Scotland came up near the wreck about sunrise, and passed without rendering assistance. According to the affidavit of the captain and crew, there was no one floating around the place at this time.

THE FIRST EXECUTION.

On the 16th of April, 1828, the public was aroused by the report of a murder committed in the Perch River settlement by Henry Evans, upon Joshua Rogers and Henry Diamond, in an affair growing out of an attempt to forcibly eject Evans without legal formality from premises leased by a brother of Rogers. A family quarrel had for some days existed in the Rogers family, in which Evans had taken a part, and at the time of the murder the parties had been drinking and were unusually quarrelsome. Evans had shut himself up in the house, which was forcibly entered, with threats and abusive language, upon which he seized an ax and mortally wounded two, and badly wounded a third, who recovered. He was immediately arrested and at the June term of the court of oyer and terminer in 1828, was tried, the court consisting of Nathan Williams, circuit judge, Egbert Ten Eyck, first judge, Joseph

Hawkins, judge, Robert Lansing, district attorney, H. H. Sherwood, clerk, H. H. Coffeen, sheriff. The district attorney was assisted by Mr. Clarke, and the prisoner was defended by Messrs. Sterling, Bronson and Rathbone. The vicious temper and abandoned character of the prisoner, who, whether drunk or sober, had been the terror of his neighborhood, outweighed the extenuating circumstances of the case, and the jury, after half an hour's deliberation, returned a verdict of guilty. He was sentenced to be hung August 22d, and he was executed in the presence of an immense crowd who had assembled to witness the barbarous spectacle from this and adjoining counties. The gallows was placed on the north bank of the river nearly opposite the court house, and thither he was escorted by a fife and drum corps. The body was taken by his friends to Brownville and a grave dug in the cemetery, when objections were raised and one person swore that he should not be buried there. Another place was then got, but the rock was reached in two feet. A grave was next dug just outside of the corporate limits, when as he was about to be lowered, objections were again raised and one or two women were seized with hysteric fits because the locality was in sight. The corpse was finally taken back three or four miles from the village and buried by night. The lamentable prevalence of superstition thus evinced, has its equal only in the popular belief in vampires, which on more than one occasion, has disgraced the annals of this and neighboring counties.

FRENCH BON VIVANTS.

Until about 1816, the settlements along the river were limited to a few points, but about this time the country around

began to be taken up; new roads were opened in every
direction, and for a short time, the country advanced rapidly
in population and improvements, which continued till the
completion of the Erie Canal. At Cape Vincent, several
educated and accomplished French families located; among
whom, in 1818, was Peter Francis Real, known in European
history as Count Real, the chief of police under Napoleon. The change of political prospects in France,
in a few years, recalled many celebrated exiles who
had adhered to the fortunes of Napoleon, and fled from
the disasters which overtook that dynasty, among whom were
Count Real, and others who had made this country their
home. At about the same time, Mr. F. R. Hasler, the eminent
philosopher and engineer, having become interested in real
estate in the place, went there to reside with his family, and
planned the establishment of a normal school, which he never
perfected. The village was a favorite resort with Mr. Le Ray,
and he was often accompanied by eminent foreigners, who
never visited the country without becoming his guests, and
sharing that refined hospitality which he knew so well how to
bestow. The first visit of Le Ray to this place was in 1803,
and was attended with the following incident:

He was accompanied by Gouverneur Morris, and after
visiting Brownville, they took an open boat to continue their
journey, as Mr. Morris had a wooden leg, and could not conveniently travel in the woods by the rude means of communication which the country then afforded, and he was moreover
very partial to sailing, and claimed to be especially skillful in
managing water craft. On passing Cherry Island, Mr. Morris
observed that there must be fine fishing there, and as he had
with him his French cook, and culinary apparatus, he
declared he would serve his friend a better fish dinner than he

had ever tasted. Mr. Le Ray objected that it was getting late and cloudy, and they had a great ways to run before reaching Putnam's, the first settlement on the shore. Nothing would do; Mr. Morris was as fond of good cheer as of sailing, and they stopped. They had good fishing, and a capital dinner; but it was late before they set sail again, and dark before they reached the St. Lawrence, and they were obliged to stop at Gravelly Point, two miles above Putnam's, where they pitched their tent and went to bed, for they had all the necessary implements. In the middle of the night, a fire built before the tent set it in flames; Mr. Morris, thus unseasonably disturbed, felt all around for his wooden leg, but was obliged to flee without it. The exposure to wind and rain produced in Mr. Le Ray a very violent illness and he with difficulty returned to Brownville. Dr. Kirkpatrick was procured from Rome, and he was long confined with a dangerous fever.

BURIED THEIR RATIONS.

There were not wanting incidents of a ludicrous kind, which enlivened the monotony of the camp, and showed the lights, as well as the shades of the soldier's life; Abuses will sometimes work their own reform, as was illustrated in an amusing instance at Sackets Harbor during the war. A mess of militia soldiers had received, for their rations, a hog's head, an article of diet not altogether available, or susceptible of fair and equal division among them. They accordingly, upon representation of the facts, procured at other messes in the cantonment, a contribution in kind, to supply their wants for the coming week, and after the morning review, having placed upon a bier, borne on the shoulders of four men, their ration of pork, they marched through the village with muffled drum, and notes of the death march, to the cemetery, where it was solemnly buried with military honors. On the next occasion, they received from the commissary store a supply of edible meat, and the occasion for a similar parade did not afterwards occur.

SEIZURE OF A CANNON.

The irritation which the events of the "Patriot War" occassioned, did not at once subside, and several of the American Steamers, especially the United States, were regarded with aversion on the Canada side for some time. As this Steamer was leaving Ogdensburg on the evening of April 14, 1839, with a large number of passengers on board, from six to ten rounds of musket shot were fired from the wharf at Prescott, upon which an angry crowd had assembled, and the same evening she was fired upon from the wharf at Brockville. A subsequent inquiry failed to fix upon any particular one as the culprits. On the 17th of May, 1839, the Schooner G. S. Weeks, stopped at Brockville to discharge some merchandise, and the usual papers were sent to the Custom House. Permission to unload was granted, when it was noticed that an iron six-pounder was lying upon deck, belonging to the State of New York, and consigned to Captain A. B. James, at Ogdensburg, being sent to replace one that had been seized by the

"Patriots" in the affair at the Windmill in the preceding year.

An attempt was made to seize this gun, which was resisted by the crew, when the Collector came up and took possession of the vessel, under the pretext of some irregularity in her papers. The gun was taken out, paraded through the streets, and fired several times by the mob in triumph. Word was sent to Colonel Worth at Sackets Harbor, who at once repaired to the scene of disturbance, and a few hours after, a steamer with British Regulars arrived from Kingston. By the united efforts of the military officers and of the civil magistrates, the gun was finally surrendered by the mob without a collision, which for a time seemed imminent and inevitable, and some of the ring-leaders were arrested and lodged in the guard-house. These disturbances brought Governor Arthur to Brockville, and an effort was made to justify these proceedings, by those who had participated in them. It is due to the Canadian Press and to the more considerate portion of the inhabitants to notice, that they very generally denounced this seizure as unjustified. The Collector was removed from office, and the irritation gradually wore away.

CHILD LOST IN THE WOODS.

The following sketch was written by Mr. David Merritt, one of the English families, who located at Sackets Harbor in February, 1805; the occasion was the loss of a child in the woods.

The parents of the child had recently settled in the woods,

half a mile from any other dwelling. It was of a Lord's day evening, about sunset; the father set out to visit his nearest neighbor, and, unobserved by him, his son, a child of four years, followed him.

The father tarried an hour or two, and returned, not having seen the little wanderer. The mother anxiously enquired for her child, supposing her husband had taken him with him; their anxiety was great, and immediate though fruitless search was made for the fugitive. Several of the nearest neighbors were alarmed, and the night was spent to no purpose in searching for the child. On Monday a more extensive search was made by increased numbers, but in vain; and the distressed parents were almost frantic with grief and fearful apprehensions for the child's safety.

Another afflictive and sleepless night passed away, and the second morning beamed upon the disconsolate family, the child not found, and by this time (Tuesday,) reports were in circulation of a panther's having been seen recently in the woods by some one. This circumstance gave a pungency to the grief and feelings of every sympathetic heart unknown before; and the timid and credulous were ready to abandon any further efforts to recover the child, and give the distressed parents up to dispair.

It was however concluded to alarm a still more extensive circle, and engage fresh volunteers in a work that must interest and arouse even the unfeeling on common occasions. A messenger was dispatched to Sackets Harbor, a distance of six miles; it was in itself an irresistible appeal to every feeling heart. To feel, was to act.

Messrs. Luff, Ashby, Merritt, and others immediately mounted their horses, and repaired to the scene of painful anxiety; this was about eleven o'clock in the forenoon of

Tuesday. When they arrived at the spot, the number present, that had collected from all quarters, was about five hundred men. A small number was immediately chosen as a committee to direct the best method of search, and they were formed in a line, extending to the right and left of the house, a mile each way. They were placed so far apart as to bring every foot of ground they passed in their search under their observation; and when they had marched such a given distance from the house, the left or right wing were to wheel in such a way, as would, by pursuing the same plan, have effectually searched every spot within several miles of the house before evening. The order of the day was that no person should fire a gun, sound a horn, halloo, or make any needless noise, whatever; but with vigilance, and a sense of duty to the distressed parents, use every effort to recover the child. If the child was found alive, every person, that had a gun, was to fire, and every one that had a horn to sound it; on the contrary, if the child was found dead, one gun only should be fired, as a signal to the remote line to cease searching.

In this way, in silence, they had marched about two miles, when a distant gun sounded; it was an anxious moment. "Is the child alive?" was a thought that ran through every mind; a moment more and the hope was confirmed, for the air and forests rang with guns and horns of every description.

The lines were immediately broken up, and each ran, anxious to see the little lost sheep. The dear little fellow was presented to his now overjoyed parents; a scene that overcame all present.

When the little boy was found, he was sitting on a small mossy hillock, in the middle of a swamp, surrounded by shallow water. When the man, who first approached him, extended his arms and stopped to take him up, he shrank from him, appeared frightened, and showed a disposition to get from him. But he was much exhausted, and seized eagerly an apple that was held to him. Had he not been rescued from his situation, he probably would have died at that spot.

FIRST LIFE SAVING STATION.

The lake shore in Ellisburgh has been the scene of many wrecks since the country was settled, the first within the memory of those living forty years ago having occurred in the fall of 1800, when a small schooner from Mexico to Gananoque, Captain Gammon, master, was lost off Little Stony Creek, and all on board perished. A boat of eight men sent in search of the vessel was also swamped and all hands were drowned.

About 1807 a family was located by Mr. Benjamin Wright at the mouth of Sandy Creek to afford aid to the shipwrecked, and for nearly fifty years this lonely dwelling had sheltered many a suffering sailor who might otherwise have perished.

A RARE BOUNTY.

The anecdote is related that a magistrate in Champion, having had an altercation with a leading citizen in Lowville, heard that his opponent had offered a bounty of $5 for his head. Feeling somewhat uneasy under this, he resolved to ascertain its truth, and made the journey on foot on purpose to demand satisfaction or a withdrawal of the offensive reward. Upon reaching the place he found the person of whom he was in search in company with several others, and not wishing to make their quarrels a subject of publicity, he requested a private interview. This was promptly refused, on the ground that there was nothing between them that required secresy, and he was told that if he had anything to say he might say it where he was. He then commenced by repeating the story he had heard and demanded whether it was true. His enemy denied at once the charge, calling his neighbors to witness whether they had ever known him guilty of the folly as the offering of such a sum, but admitted that he might have bid twenty shillings and was very sure he had never gone higher. Finding that it was impossible to get this bounty taken off he returned home. We are not informed of the result or whether the reward was sufficient to tempt the cupidity of his neighbors.

MILITARY EXECUTIONS.

At Sackets Harbor about a dozen military executions were performed during the war, for repeated desertion, with the view of striking terror into the minds of the disaffected, but with the effect of increasing the evil. These cases were many of them young men from New England, of respectable families, who in the heat of political excitement had enlisted in the army, and who found themselves the victims of the wanton barbary of officers, exposed to the severest hardships of the camp, and often illy clad, and worse fed, sometimes without shelter, and always without sympathy. Was it unnatural that under these circumstances the memories of home, with all its comforts, and the thoughts of mothers, sisters, wives, and children, and the thousand associations that cluster around the domestic fireside, should come freshly to mind with a force that was irresistible? Several of these cases excited much sympathy, among which was that of a boy of sixteen years of age, who had been bribed with a gold watch, to open a prison door at Greenbush, and who was here arrested and convicted. Many officers and citizens made strenuous efforts to obtain reprieve, which were enforced by the appeals of a mother, but without effect; the agonized parent followed her child to the gallows, and the sympathizing tears of the spectators bespoke the feeling which this rigid exercise of the iron rule of war had occasioned.

To the condemned opportunity was always given to make remarks, in which some admitted the justice of their fate, others plead the entreaties of their comrades, or the urgent necessities of home; and others, while they acknowledged their crime, supplicated mercy with all the eloquence which the occasion could command. Others treated their fate with indifference, or openly preferred it to a life under the circumstances. On one occasion, the convict on approaching the scaffold, scrutinized its construction with the eye of a carpenter, leaped upon the platform, pushed off the hangman, and jumped off himself; but a reprieve arrived the instant after, and he was restored. The place of execution was generally in the rear of the village, where the graves were dug, and the convicts were marched to the spot, surrounded by a guard, and after kneeling by their coffins, were dispatched by the shots of

of several muskets, a part of which only were loaded with ball.
There were commonly eight men detailed for this purpose.
The brutality of officers was in some instances excessive; the
most extreme corporal punishment being inflicted from the
slightest causes, or from mere caprice; and such was sometimes the bitterness of men towards officers, that in one case it
is said a captain durst not lead his company in an action, for
fear of being shot by his own men.

THEY CELEBRATED.

The first celebration of our national independence, in all
this region of country, was held at Chaumont in 1802. The
number in attendance was certainly more than a hundred
persons. From Champion and Hounsfield, Watertown and
Brownville, Sackets Harbor and Cape Vincent, and other
points of settlement, the forefathers and foremothers came to
do homage to the old flag and the land of the brave. Several
were Revolutionary soldiers. Food and drink were plenty.
Indians and squaws must also have joined the festivities.
Rum and maple sugar, shooting at a mark and wrestling,
stories and songs, and fife and drum, could hardly have been
wanting on this occasion, although there is no published report of the proceedings to guide in making out the history of
that Fourth of July.

BLOCKHOUSE—SCHOOLHOUSE.

Considerable alarm was felt at Chaumont in 1812 lest the
British should come, pillage their homes and burn them;

nor did they know but hostile Indians might take advantage
of the war to pounce upon them and carry off their scalps.
General Brown therefore advised the building of a blockhouse for defense, and this was erected the same year, on the
north shore of the bay. Not long after, a squad of English
soldiers visited the place, and promised not to destroy any
property if the inhabitants would take down the blockhouse.
This was done, and the material afterwards rafted to Point
Salubrious and used in the erection of a building for school
and religious purposes, but long since demolished. The
artillery of this "fort" consisted of an iron gun which
Jonas Smith had purchased some time before for two
gallons of rum. It was found on the isthmus of Point Peninsula. Afterwards this gun was taken to Sackets Harbor
and form thence to Ogdensburg, where it was captured by the
enemy.

A Past Industry.

The fisheries of Chaumont Bay afforded from an early period a leading pursuit for many persons living in the vicinity and have been productive of much benefit to the locality and the public generally. The earliest enactment relating to this branch of industry commences with the century. It having been represented that people from Canada and other places were doing injustice to the fisheries at the east end of Lake Ontario by obstructing the rivers and streams by seines, a law was passed March 28th, 1800, prohibiting the placing of obstructions to the passage of fish under a penalty of $25. This was probably from representations of citizens in Ellisburgh as Lyme was then without inhabitants.

In 1808 fishing with scoop nets, called here scaff nets begun, wrote Dr. Hough in 1853, and has been more or less constantly practiced since. This net is about 12 feet square, stretched by two long bows crossing each other and let down horizontally into the water, being balanced on a long pole poised on a post on the banks. When fish pass over it the net is suddenly raised and swung round on the bank. Sometimes 300 fish or more are thus caught in a night. [Whitefish and salmon trout were taken in great quantities by this crude method on Point Salubrious.] Seines were soon after introduced, the first one being brought from the Hudson by Daniel Tremper. These seines are from 10 to 100 rods long, from 20 to 100 feet broad, wider in the middle and narrower at the ends, where they are attached to rods called jack stakes. To the cords along one side are attached floats and to the other leaden sinkers and to each staff is fixed a long rope. When used the seine is taken out in a boat one rope being left on shore, and when a few rods out it is allowed to run off in a wide circuit until it is all off, when the other line is taken ashore and both ends are drawn in by windlasses erected for the purpose and turned by hand, or more recently sometimes by horse power. The meshes of the net which are from one to one and one-half inches square, allow the smaller fish to escape, while the larger ones are scooped out when the seine is drawn into shallow water. From one to three hours are occupied in drawing the seine and the product of a haul varies from nothing to 75 barrels, the average being six or seven.

These seine fisheries are mostly around Point Salubrious but other places inside of the bay are found eligible to a less extent. They are considered the property of those who own the adjacent lands and the seines are owned and labor done by the resident farmers assisted by laborers who come in from adjacent towns for the purpose. The principal fish caught for market are lake herring, locally known as ciscoes, and whitefish, and the season for taking them usually begins about the first of November and continued three or four weeks. This is the spawning season for these fish and the shores are then lined with immense quantities of their ova. Seines are drawn by preference in the evening or night.

No positive data can be obtained showing the average or

aggregate quantity taken, but the opinion of those most acquainted with the business is that since 1816 about 10,000 barrels of herring and white fish have been caught annually. Seasons vary in the abundance of fish; it is observed that the best yields occur in high water. Of late years the yield is less than formerly, which is attributed to the use of gill nets and the mixture of saw dust and other matters in the water.

Gill nets have been introduced since 1845, are from five to eight feet, (about fifty meshes) wide, from ten to fifteen rods long, uniform in width and furnished with staves at the ends. These are provided with sinkers on the lower and floats on the upper side and connected together form lines several hundred rods long. When in use they lay near the bottom and their places are indicated by buoys. Once daily they are drawn up and the fish removed, which sometimes amount to a barrel in ten rods. As the fish become entangled by their gills, respiration ceases, and they are almost invariably found drowned, for which reason they are justly considered inferior for food and more liable to spoil when put up for sale. These nets are generally set in November.

A small business was done early in spring, in fishing for pike in seines, gill nets and by spearing, and the shores and coves of Chaumont Bay have long been the favorite resort for the disciples of Izaak Walton, who at most seasons find an ample and inviting field for the use of the trolling line and spear; or a romantic cruise by torchlight and inducements to lounge away the lazy hours of daylight with reasonable hopes of a nibble. Pike, pickerel, muscallonge, perch, bass and sunfish, are caught readily by the hook and the former in all seasons. The seines used here are generally made on the spot of linen or cotton twine and cost from $100 to $300.

In 1817, April 15, a law was passed requiring all fish barreled for sale in the county to be inspected and branded and the size of barrels and quantity of salt to be used were prescribed. In 1823, April 13, another law relating to this subject was passed; March 8, 1830, an additional inspector was appointed, and April 15, 1835, the inspection of fish was discontinued. Calvin Lincoln was appointed inspector June 11, 1817, M. Evans, March 19, 1818, and Benjamin T. Bliss on Point Salubrious afterwards. The early laws were disregarded, but the latter strictly enforced, yet the restriction was always considered odious by the fishermen who sought many ways of evasion and finally procured their removal.

By far the most successful fishing in Chaumont bay has been with the pound-net. This method of fishing was introduced in the spring of 1859 by Ralph H. Rogers, the son of a Revolutionary soldier who was one of three brothers in the Bunker Hill engagement, and himself a veteran of the war of 1812. He set a pound-net off the shore of Point Peninsula, and about the middle of October another was set by O. H. Kirtland, Lucius P. Ingram, and D. W. Clark, who came on from Saybrook, Connecticut, for the purpose. The yields were enormous for the next two or three years, and it was sometimes impossible to care for the fish which were caught.

The average size of the pound-net is 30 feet square, and it is usually set in about 30 feet of water, although nets to fish in 40 feet were not unusual. This is securely fastened to four stakes driven firmly into the bottom, with the upper ends two or three feet out of water. From this pound or receiver, towards the shore, is a large heart-shaped net, with the apex terminating in the pound. From the base of the heart a leader is run back to the shore, and fastened to stakes a hundred feet apart; the average length of the leader is thirteen hundred feet, and the stakes, as in the other instance, are firmly driven into the bottom of the bay. The fish meet this long line of netting, follow it down into the heart, and work towards the apex, because of its peculiar shape. At the apex is a large funnel, with a large passage out of the heart, and a smaller one at the outer end, which terminates in the pound or receiver. After the fish have once passed through the funnel into the large square pound—reaching from the surface of the water to the bottom of the bay,—the chances of escape are very small. From a net of this kind a hundred barrels of fish have been taken at one time. They are now little used except for taking spawn for the state hatcheries.

Three Links.

Over the signature of "A Link in the Chain," Mr. Solon Massey of Watertown, contributed many entertaining anecdotes of the earlier settlers which were published in the Jeffersonian, 1851-52. The three following are selected for this volume:

LOST IN THE WOODS.

To any person who realizes what a dense howling wilderness this country was at the time of its first occupation by our fathers, it will not be surprising that there were instances rather frequent, of persons being lost in the woods.

The natural divisions of hill and dale, or upland and lowland, in this comparative level country, afforded but few landmarks to the unlucky wight who happened to get at fault in his reckonings, and even those who were best acquainted with the natural scenery of the trackless forest, immediately surrounding our settlement, were sometimes compelled to experience the startling reality of being lost in the woods; which was indicated by finding themselves following a circle—coming round and round and round again, to the same starting point, in spite of all their efforts to follow out a continuous straight course.

This liability to be lost was so well understood, that

whenever any member of the family was longer away in the forest than was expected, the alarm was given, and a rally made of all the men and boys in the different settlements in the vicinity, and a general and systematic search instituted with preconcerted signals.

And yet even the liability to get lost did not deter or prevent frequent intercourse with the woods. The forest was the "long pasture" where the cows lived in summer, and where they had to be hunted over long ranges of upland, or of swale and beaver meadow, as their fancy or necessity led them to forage for themselves. It was the botanic garden where a long list of medicinal plants were found, which were relied upon as preventives of the diseases that were incident to our new country, or as a sovereign balm for every wound with which we might be afflicted for the time being. It was the place for berrying for a great variety of fruits and berries in their season the great range from which we hunted out our natural-crook scythe snaths, our crotched trees for harrows and cart tongues, our ax halves, ox yoke and ox-bow timber, broom sticks, etc.; and finally, it was the great hunting ground for a variety of wild game, with which to supply our tables with meat, in the absence of domestic animals for food. Woods was the rule, clearings the exception.

One incident among a great many others, connected with being lost in the woods, may be transcribed from the earliest traditional history of Watertown, and which is something as follows:

Capt. James Parker owned and occupied a large body of land (now a farm) on the Brownville road, at present occupied in part by his son James. He had a large family of sturdy boys, the oldest of whom, at the time our tradition dates, was fourteen to sixteen years of age. The old gentleman, like many others of our enterprising settlers, was clearing up a large farm, and, for the purpose of making the most out of his ashes, had a small potash works, where he worked them into potash or black salts.

In the process of manufacture, it seems he wanted some hemlock gum, and at the same time wanted some groceries from the little place yclepted a store here in the village. So handing the hero of our story a silver dollar, he bid him take his ax and a bag, and on his way to or from the store to procure some gum. With this errand and equipment he started, after dinner, on his way to the place; he proceeded as far as the foot of the Folts Hill (H. H. Coffeen's late residence,) where, stretching away to the south was an abundance of hemlock timber, and intent on performing the hardest and most difficult part of his task first, and not wishing to risk losing his dollar, he struck his ax into a large tree and loosening a chip he carefully deposited the coin in the cavity between the loosened chip and the body of the tree for safe keeping, intending to come back to that starting point with his ax and bag, and leave them there in their turn, while he ran up to the store and back.

Well, after a while he found himself sufficiently provided with gum, and started off a kind of Indian lope for the place where he had left the dollar, passing in his way a spring of water, upon the surface of which was a thick yellow scum, resembling iron rust. On, on, on he traveled, sweating under his load, and with the lurking suspicion that something was wrong, he didn't know what. After a good while, however, and when he knew he must have traveled more than any distance that could possibly have been between the last gum tree and the one containing his dollar, he made a full halt for the purpose of a reckoning. One thing was very certain—that he had traveled faster coming back than when going, and had been longer about it. That had a bad look! then he thought it curious there should have been three of those iron ore springs, looking so nearly alike! And finally, the more he soliloquized the more he satisfied himself that he was lost.

What added not a little to his perplexity was, that twilight was already spreading her mantle upon the forest. It would therefore be necessary for him to select where he would spend the night, so far as there was any choice of a sheltered place in the woods. He was not long in finding a large standing tree that afforded just the nook he wanted, between two roots that stood well out on either side, and having ensconced himself in a sitting posture, with his back against the tree, and the ax between his knees, he prepared to face any danger that might offer, and to sleep away the long hours of the night. He would have telegraphed the folks at home that he was safe, if he could. He hoped they would not be much alarmed. But they were though, and after sunset the old gentleman got uneasy and started out the way that he should come, just to meet him—if he was safe—but with a kind of presentment, to succor him if in trouble. He kept on, occasionally stopping to listen, and sweating with his apprehension, and imagining a whole catalogue of mishaps that might have befallen him—whether he had lost his way—or had maimed himself with the ax— or a tree had fallen upon him—or, what was certainly possible, some ravenous wild beast had devoured him—all was a matter of painful doubt, fear, an uncertainty.

It was not, however, until after he had reached the village, and found by enquiry that his boy had not been there, that his fearful forebodings of some horrible evil were confirmed.

Giving the alarm here, and begging of the good people to

rally quickly and meet such persons as he should succeed in obtaining from Brownville, he hastened home in such a state of mind as can be better imagined than described.

Until his arrival home, the family had not partaken very much of his own alarm, but now, what a sad and sorrowful company are they, as hurriedly they make the necessary preparation, with pine knots and birch bark for torches, horns and guns for signals, and refreshments for the missing boy if he should be found, and for the kind neighbors who were in all probability to be in the woods all night.

In due time, a large company of men and boys were assembled, and having organized into bands, with preconcerted signals, they struck off into the forest, while the mother and sisters of the missing boy sat in the open door of their lonely tenement to await the slow and tedious result, and so as to be in a situation to catch the first sound of any signal guns announcing the fate of him they loved.

Thus passed the first half of the night. The hunt proceeded with great fidelity, so that every rod of the ground was inspected, the horns sounding at regular intervals of time, so as to preserve the line of march, or to catch the ear of the boy if preadventure he was alive.

The party had proceeded on carefully, until within a few rods of where the hero of the play kept his night vigil, before his dreams were disturbed and he sufficiently awake to know that it was for his benefit that the horns were sounded; but when fairly awake, he was not long in vacating his quiet retreat, and arresting the further progress of the search, by presenting himself in propria personae, with his ax on his shoulder and gum bag under his arm, before the satisfied cavalcade.

Bang! bang! bang! rang out in quick succession upon

the night air, reverberating to each extremity of the long line of weary hunters, the preconcerted signal which notified the quick ear of the listening mother and sisters that Ellick was safe. There was more joy manifested that night over the boy that was found than over all them that went not astray.

A MAN SHOT BY HIS FRIEND.

In the fall of 1801, there was a man, whose name was Dayton, who obtained a contract for a piece of land lying south of the road to Brownville, as you climb the Folts Hill. He built a small log house in the woods, near the present road, and was keeping bachelor's hall, through the months of September and October of that year, with no other companion than a young man who was a brother to his wife. He was intending to remove his family here in the spring, but, as it turned out, he lacked the fortitude and courage which were requisite for pioneer life.

While thus living, an event occurred, which, for the time being, quickened the pulses of the entire community, and which seemed more like tragedy than any previous occurrence in our brief history.

There was a project for a squirrel hunt, among the scattered inhabitants of the several neighborhoods, and Dayton and his brother-in-law were expecting to participate in the general war against the squirrels and other vermin, who were likely to get more than a fair proportion of the first corn crop ever cultivated in these wilds—though they themselves had no cornfields. And here we remark by the way, how unselfish

men become, as soon as they get beyond the old settlements.
Mutual dependence soon exerts a softening influence upon the
human heart, and the sympathies flow out without stint as
often as the sufferings present themselves for aid or sympathy.
This, probably, is the clue to that proverbial happiness, which
in all ages and in all countries, dates back to the pioneer settlements in a new country.

With the purpose of having his gun in readiness for the
approaching hunt, Mr. Dayton took it down one evening, from
its place over-head, and sitting down before the blazing fire,
laid it across his knees, preparatory to taking off the lock and
oiling its pinions, so as to insure a smart motion of the hammer
spring. He was not aware that it contained a full charge of
powder and shot, or that it was loaded at all; but carelessly
held the muzzle towards his friend, who was sitting in the
other corner of the fire-place, keeping up a cheerful light, by
timely contributions of light, dry combustibles, to the open
fire. It is probable that he pulled the trigger without thought
or motive; but what was his horror and amazement when his
piece discharged with a report that was almost deafening,
filling the room with smoke, and then he heard his companion
fall to the floor, exclaiming " I am shot! I am shot!"

They had no light but the open fire, and the smoke was
so thick and suffocating that no examination could be made.
It was all uncertain, what the extent of the injury might be;
but knowing that Doctor Isaiah Massey had recently arrived
from Vermont to share our fortunes with us, and that he was
boarding at our village tavern, it was agreed that Dayton
should find his way through the dark pine woods which intervened, and bring the doctor.

My father had some corn collected from his field, and with
the male members of his family—kind men and boarders—

doctor included, was in the house (log barn,) husking; and my mother was keeping her night vigils alone in the house, when her ear detected the quick, hurried step of Mr. Dayton, as he rushed into the door, exclaiming, "I have killed my brother, and want the doctor!" As soon as he was sufficiently composed to state his case understandingly, he was directed to the husking party, for the doctor, while my mother, as if by instinct, set herself about preparing some clean linen rags, for bandages and lint, and some tallow candles for lights, with which our young Esculapius was soon on his way, on horseback and alone, to answer to the first case of surgery and gun shot wounds which had presented itself in his pioneer practice.

He was evidently a good deal flurried, as he struck into the woods in advance of his guide, to endeavor to thread his dubious way; and he was frequently heard to say, afterwards, that it was the greatest trial his nerves had ever endured.

For aught he knew (and in the circumstances of the case, as narrated by the affrighted Dayton, a thing quite probable), his patient was already dead, and stiffened in his gore, an object frightful enough, to be visited alone, by broad day light; how much more, in the dim light of any embers which might be left in that lonely house in the woods.

His near approach to the house, which he after awhile succeeded in finding, did not alleviate his feelings much; for now, the case must be met, whatever may be its developments. The idea of stumbling over a dead man, in his efforts to strike a light, or of groping about the room in search of a mutilated human being, was all his nerves would bear, and he trembled in his stirrups.

He however grew ashamed of his fear, and after listening

a moment at the door, tapped gently for admission; there was
no answer. He lifted the latch and pressed his weight
against the door, but it was fastened on the inside. He
knocked again. "Who is there?" said the young man. "The
doctor." "Wait a minute and I will open the door," said he,
as he crawled off his couch and proceeded to take away the
barricade with which he had fastened the door. He apologized
for the delay by saying that he had heard that wolves were
attracted by the smell of blood, and that finding himself
bleeding pretty profusely, he had thought it prudent to fasten
himself in.

It proved to be a case of no imminent danger, after all.
The charge of shot from the gun had penetrated the fleshy
part of the thigh of the young man, and after a proper dressing, for which the forethought of my mother had amply
provided them, the young doctor mounted his horse and returned to the village, where he soon succeeded in allaying the
fears of the community, by his professional opinion that he
would recover, with proper care.

A WOLF STORY OF EARLY TIMES.

In the brief history that I wrote out for your paper two
or three weeks ago, from the early traditions of our town,
describing a scene, which was almost a tragedy, between Mr.
Dayton and his brother-in-law, at the foot of the Folts Hill,
on the Brownville road, I stated, that the wounded man had
taken the precaution to fasten his door on the inside, so as to

prevent the ingress of wolves that might be attracted by the smell of blood, while Mr. Dayton was after the doctor.

I know it is somewhat difficult for the present generation to comprehend the situation of peril in which scattering families were placed at that early day, or that there was any real and positive danger of molestation by the wolves; and therefore, I shall transcribe another incident, in the traditions of early man and early times, which will tend to correct any doubts upon that subject.

The late Hon. Jotham Ives was among the early emigrants into this town. He arrived here in 1801, and located his home, where he lived to amass a large landed property, and where he died, recently, near the place called Field Settlement.

In the fall of 1802, he had a number of hogs fattened, and at killing time he employed a Mr. Knowlton, an old, white-haired man of sixty years or more, who was somewhat skilled in butchering, to assist him. Knowlton lived about three-fourths of a mile from Mr. Ives, in the near neighborhood of the present residence of Mr. James Brintnall, where he had a little clearing, or what was perhaps more appropriately called, in backwoods phrase, a chopping, and which was surrounded by a temporary brush fence. Between himself and Mr. Ives there was no road; and nothing but a line of marked trees to designate the little footpath which meandered through the deep, dark, and in many places tangled forest, which stretched off almost interminably on either hand.

The butchering over, and supper disposed of, it was agreed that there was time to cut up the pork, and Mr. Knowlton consented to stay and assist in doing so. At a late hour, the whole work was finally completed, and Mr.

Knowlton was generously compensated for his valued services in addition to which he was made welcome to a couple of hogs' plucks to carry home to his family.

But as he was about to leave for home, Mrs. Ives suggested the hazard of passing through the woods at that late hour, with the smell of blood upon his clothes, and invited him to stay all night; to which Knowlton answered that he could not think of being away from his family all night as they would be alarmed for his safety, being unable to account for his absence; that, as for the wolves, though they might prowl around his path they would not dare to molest him.

Now Mr. Ives was a man of great muscular power and would not fear a regiment of wolves himself, and though he assured Mr. Knowlton that he might stay in welcome, yet he scouted the idea of danger from the sneaking cowardly wolves, and advised him, however, that in case he should be followed by them to leave the plucks for them to quarrel over while he should hurry on home.

The colloquy being ended, Knowlton finally took his leave with a pluck in each hand and struck into the woods to endeavor to follow out his little foot path. He had not proceeded, far, however, before a sharp and startling sound, a fearful howl, rang out upon the night air evidently betokening the near neighborhood of a prowling wolf on his right, which was answered from another quarter, and then another in quick succession, until the path, that he had traveled but a moment before seemed to be alive with hungry seekers after blood.

He had yet no fears for his personal safety and had no thought of cowardice, but yet he confessed that there was something dismal in the thought of being alone and entirely unarmed at such a time in such a place groping and feeling his dubious way in such close proximity to a pack of ravenous wild beasts, and he soon found himself quickening his pace, while ever and anon he instinctively cast a wistful eye over his shoulder and into the recesses of the thick woods on either hand.

It was not long, however, that any doubt remained about his being the object of their pursuit, as his quick ear detected the galloping movement of a troop of pattering feet on his track, and it was becoming more and more a question of interest with him how the chase would terminate.

He hoped when he reflected that he was nearing his own habitation every moment and his path was becoming plainer, and he was able to make better progress. But the odds was with them for they were lighter of foot and could see a great deal better than he could in the gloom of the forest, but, more than all, they were so many and were mad with hunger and were becoming more and more desperate every moment. On, on, on, the old man strode resolutely and with a strength and speed which would have surprised him at any other time, even by daylight, but which seemed slow enough now in the time of his extremity.

If he could but keep them at bay a little longer and until he could clear the dark woods and get the benefit of the comparatively open light of his chopping, or lay his hand upon a strong hand spike, sled stake or billet of wood, he might still hope to defend himself successfully or escape from their hungry jaws. Straining every nerve he bounded onward with such agility as only desperation and love of life afforded ; but the distance between him and his pursuers was not lessened by all his efforts. and before he reached the brush fence that surrounded his peaceful home he felt that his time had nearly come, when he bethought himself of the parting advice of his friend Ives.

He acted upon the suggestion and immediately hurled one of the plucks into their midst ; in the next moment he was on the home side of his brush fence and they were fighting over the paltry price with which he had purchased his own safety. It may be safely assumed that he did not wait to witness the result of the civil war which he had occasioned, but that as soon as possible he found himself on the inside of his rude domicile, with the door fastened on the inside.

Mr. Knowlton lived many years after the event which I have narrated and died a natural death, and the woods which were the scene of our story have long since been cleared away and the wolves are only known as figuring in the history of the olden time.

A Bit of Topography.

The foregoing ingenious chart was prepared by Mr. Frederick Campbell of Lowville, and was accompanied by the following interesting data :

The topography of the country traversed between Utica and the Thousand Islands is to most people entirely unknown. The grades are so met that most tourists would be quite unconscious that there were any marked grades at all ; and many would exhibit no surprise if they should be told that no higher elevations above sea level are met between Utica and the Thousand Islands than between New York and Utica. The accompanying cut, which I have carefully prepared from official reports will reveal the facts.

In the chart each space represents 100 feet above sea level ; the irregular line thus makes graphic the elevations of the entire route. At the left are given the elevations of a number of places in the United States with which the elevations of places on the Thousand Island route may be compared.

It will here be seen that the climb from New York to Utica is insignificant : there is a rise of only 32 feet in passing from New York to Albany, though the distance is nearly 150 miles.

ELEVATIONS ABOVE SEA LEVEL

FROM UTICA TO 1,000 ISLANDS VIA R.W. AND O.RR., COMPARED WITH ELEVATIONS OF OTHER PROMINENT PLACES

A BIT OF TOPOGRAPHY

And at 238 miles from New York, Utica is found at an elevation of only 410 feet above the sea. But one has proceeded only 16 miles on the Rome, Watertown and Ogdensburg railroad (Black River division) when he has doubled his elevation, (Trenton,) and with thirteen miles more (Alder Creek) has multiplied it by three. While the summit level of the Black River canal is at Boonville, at an elevation of 1,119 feet, the summit of the Black River route is found a little to the south of Alder Creek, the latter place itself being 1,245 feet above the sea. From that point it is a steady decline to Martinsburg station, the descent being particularly swift between Boonville and Port Leyden, the passenger being able to note it by watching the locks of the parallel canal. In seven miles there is a drop of 235 feet, the first three miles of the distance taking 145 feet of the drop. From Martinsburg it will be seen that there is another climb to Lowville, 845 feet elevation, whence there is a practically continuous down grade to Clayton, which, at 232 feet elevation is but little more than half that of Utica.

Referring to the comparative figures on the left, it will be observed that the elevation of Utica is midway between that of Harrisburg, Pa., and Rochester, 310 and 510 respectively. Holland Patent stands 30 feet higher than Chicago. Trenton is much higher than either St. Paul or Kansas City, and but little less than Topeka, Kans. Trenton Falls is 45 feet higher than Fargo, N. D., Remsen exceeds the celebrated Altoona on the Pennsylvania railroad by 24 feet, and Alder Creek is within 35 feet of being as high as Chautauqua lake, which boasts the highest navigated water east of the Rocky mountains. Boonville is 100 feet higher than Omaha, Lowville is nearly even with Topeka, Carthage with Kansas City, and Clayton with Schenectady.

The French Settlers.

The following paper is from the pen of Mrs. M. L. Whitcher of Whitesboro, N. Y.:

Those who like to wander in the by-paths of our nation's history will remember that at a very early period of the revolution Dr. Franklin being sent in 1777 as ambassador to the French court to gain the assistance of that government in carrying on our war with England, was tendered and accepted the use of a villa at Passy, rent free, by its owner a wealthy banker. Dr. Franklin occupied the villa nine years.

This act of generous hospitality was done by Monsieur M. Le Ray de Chaumont, who was a student of the affairs of the struggling colonies and deeply interested in the cause of liberty. He gave Dr. Franklin a warm reception and, as the American commissioners could not be openly received by the French court, he gave up his seat in the ministry that he might act as intermediary between the Americans and his own government.

He became the friend and patron of the colonists and sent them a whole cargo of powder with instructions that it need not be paid for unless their cause was won. We recently

learned from the agent of the Le Ray estate that the powder so generously furnished had not been paid for. The cargo consisted of two thousand barrels. From his own purse M. Le Ray also fitted a ship to join the Bon Homme Richard and was chosen to superintend the equipment of the entire squadron which was destined to cast lustre on the name of John Paul Jones.

M. James Donatius Le Ray, the banker's eldest son, was at this time completing his education, studying English with his father's venerable friend, Dr. Franklin. He, too, became interested in American affairs and visited this country soon after the revolution, bearing letters of introduction from Dr. Franklin to Gouverneur Morris, DeWitt Clinton and other prominent men. During a second visit he bought large tracts of land, one in New Jersey and another in Otsego county, this state, for which Judge Cooper, father of the novelist, J. Fennimore Cooper, was his agent. But the largest of his purchases was a tract of two hundred and twenty thousand acres of land in Jefferson county, the most of which was bought on Jan. 3, 1803, from William Constable, the grandfather of the late Hon. William C. Pierrepont of Pierrepont Manor. It was on this property that he built his home. A hamlet sprung up around his grand mansion, named Le Raysville, as the township was very properly called Le Ray. The homestead site and hamlet are near the line of the Utica and Black River railroad, the nearest station, Felts Mills, being only three miles distant. Its sole claim to public notice, aside from the air of historical romance still clinging to it, is the picturesque beauty of its scenery. The original dwelling built in 1810, was burned in 1822. This was replaced by a mansion which was completed in 1827, and stands on the original site, a plateau of ten acres, from which the ground falls away on every side. Its walls of massive stone are covered with stucco similar to that which adorns the White House at Washington. The house is two stories high, with wings at either side and a large basement. Four large rooms occupy each floor, the front parlors and corresponding rooms above being octagon in form. One of the wings was used as a chapel and the other for a library. In the basement were the storerooms, pantries, kitchen and wine cellar. The floor of the last mentioned is of stone, while all around the sides were shelves so arranged with holes that the wines, always the choicest variety, were kept on their corks. A number of wine casks are still standing in the old cellar and the aroma, which is even at this time plainly perceptible, is a vivid reminder of the times when the mansion was widely famous for its frequent and generous hospitality. Among the many distinguished guests entertained at the mansion were Gouverneur Morris, Governor Clinton and President Monroe, who, shortly after his inauguration, made a tour of the northern frontier to inspect the military fortifications and learn their strength in case of need. The president arrived in August, 1817, and remained for several days, the guest of M. Le Ray. The president wore the undress uniform of an officer of the revolution—a military coat, light colored breeches and a cocked hat.

In the grand octagon parlors there are still some of the massive elegant pier tables, with their plate glass backs and carved lions' feet, while above the marble mantels are the grand old mirrors extending to the ceiling, and at either side are elegant bronze chandeliers, which supported large clusters of wax candles. The walls of these rooms are still without spot or blemish although they were finished in 1827. To one visitor, at least, who would tell the story of their hey-dey and their desolation there is an indescribable charm in these—

THE FRENCH SETTLERS.

"Rooms of luxury and state,
That old magnificence so richly furnished,
With cabinet of ancient date
And carvings gilt and burnished."

The mansion faces the forest. On its left was the deer park, where tame fawns might be seen quietly grazing, while to the right were the ample gardens, which were famous for rare fruits and choice flowers and vegetables, imported from France or furnished from the gardens at the White House in Washington, their only superior in this country.

A neat bridge with white latticed railing still spans the stream that runs in front of the mansion and forms an attractive feature of the landscape from the piazza, where the massive Doric columns extend to the roof. "Where once the garden smiled" is now a field of wheat. The old garden walks can now only be traced by some lilac or sturdy rose. The beautiful grave beside the garden is still standing and through it the old path leads to the waterfall and the ruins of what was once a pretty alcove. Of the many arbors, rustic bowers and summer houses which were arranged so invitingly about the grounds, only one remains, the spy-house, an octagon structure, neatly plastered and painted. This cozy retreat was furnished with books, papers and a spy-glass, with which the members of the household could amuse themselves with watching the movements of the villagers. Between the spy-house and the village was an artificial pond formed by damming the stream which murmured through the ground at the waterfall only to appear again near the mansion. The sheet of water is called St. James' lake. It was stocked with speckled trout and provided with pleasure boats. It still furnishes the young villagers a fine boating place.

The waterfall is a place of wild, romantic beauty. The

waters of the stream which murmurs through the grove here plunge down a deep, rocky chasm and disappear from sight. At the foot of the chasm is a small cave where the sunshine never enters, but above and around it wild flowers bloom profusely. The air seems always filled with the music of song birds, odors of wild flowers and the soft splashing of the falling water. It seems like enchanted ground.

In the grove near the fall is the tomb of a little child. It is covered by a slab of gray marble and upon an upright stone one may read: "Here lies Clotilde de Gouvello, died Sept. 20, 1818. She was endeared to her parents and tenderly loved by all who watched her thirteen months of patient suffering life. Strew flowers upon her grave, but weep not, for she numbers with angels in Heaven." This little one was the grandchild of M. LeRay and was the only one of the family who was buried in America. She was baptized in the grove not far from her last quiet resting place. A huge boulder, which presented a large flat surface about four feet from the ground, was, with candles, crucifix and fair linen, transformed into an altar. A large branch of a tall oak spread out protectingly as a canopy over it, and near the end of the limb two of its smaller branches suggested the antlers of a deer. Artistic carving of the end of the limb completed a close resemblance to a deer's head. At its neck was hung a bell which could be rung from the ground by means of a nicely adjusted rope and pulley. On a pleasant afternoon in August, 1817, at a given hour, the bell was rung, and the family, accompanied by servants, sponsors and priest, marched in quiet procession to the appointed place. When the solemn sacrament of baptism had been administered to the child the party returned to the mansion where a baptismal feast had been prepared, and gifts, to commemorate the event,

were distributed to all the retainers of the household. The
mother of this child was Therese, only daughter of M. LeRay.
She had remained in France, where she became engaged in
marriage to the Marquis De Gouvello. Her father had been
sent for to assist in drawing up the marriage settlements and
when that important document was read the daughter
demanded a change, providing that, in case of divorce, her
portion of her husband's estate should be doubled. Her father
remonstrated, declaring that God, who ordained marriage,
designed the union to be perpetual, and would not bless a
bond accepted by the lips when the heart harbored thoughts
of its severance. The marriage was therefore postponed until
the judgment of the daughter harmonized with that of her
father. It was in honor of this daughter that the town of
Theresa was named, as Cape Vincent was named for his son
Vincent, Alexandria Bay for his son Alexander, Juhelville
(now a part of Watertown) for his mother-in-law, and Plessis
was named for his dog.

In his religion, M. Le Ray was a devout Catholic, yet
liberal in his spiritual as he was generous in his material
things. This was shown in his gifts of land and building
materials for the building of churches of any denomination.
He also contributed freely for the establishment of schools.
In fact in all of his affairs he used very liberal measures.

He sent agents to France and other countries circulated
pamphlets and sought to induce those who had been neighbors in the old world to unite in settling the new. He
brought gentlemen of education and ability to superintend
the establishing of mills and factories which he provided as
the wants of the settlers required. These gentlemen brought
with them not only the arts and industries of the higher
civilization of their old home, but somewhat more of the idea

of social rank and dignity of position that was used in new American settlements, in the northern states at least. For, although the family and all their household were courteous and conciliatory, this did not bridge over the great social gulf between them and their neighbors, and when the great family carriage bowled through the village the housekeepers left their baking and churning to catch a glimpse of the passing grandeur. "There's such divinity doth hedge a king." These people furnished a denial to that popular fallacy "that all men are created equal."

Prominent among the distinguished French gentlemen who purchased land of M. Le Ray was Joseph Bonaparte, ex-king of Spain. After the defeat at Waterloo in 1815, Joseph, realizing that "riches have wings," offered M. Le Ray, who was then in France (where he had been sent to settle some accounts between that government and the United States,) several wagon loads of silver for an uncertain amount of his American territory. There were no surveys or title deeds agreed upon, as the Bonapartes were in great haste to get out of France and there was little time for details. Napoleon promised to meet his brother in this country and there is no doubt, that had the emperor been allowed to select his own line of travel, he would have preferred to live with his marshals and generals on our northern frontier to the lonely isle of St. Helena.

Joseph Bonaparte made a purchase of one hundred and twenty thousand acres in Jefferson and Lewis counties. A beautiful lake on the edge of the North Woods is still called Bonaparte Lake. In extent it is more than a thousand acres; it is dotted with picturesque islands, and being fed wholly by subterranean streams its waters have a wonderful clearness, such as has made Loches Lomond and Katrine famous in Scottish history.

At a place on Indian river about nine miles from the village of Carthage, the waters flow under a rock of white limestone, and at this point, called Natural Bridge, Joseph Bonaparte built a house in 1829, which is still standing. The bridge on the upper side is nearly as smooth as masonry, while beneath, the waters have worn deep grottoes where one may walk upright into the rocky recesses until he finds himself groping into darkness. This locality rewards the seeker of specimens of rocks and minerals. The near-by Bonaparte house might easily be mistaken for an old-fashioned meeting house without belfry or steeple. It is now a tenement, but its occupants still take pride in showing its oddities to the curious visitors and in furnishing their own admiring commentary upon the former owner, the count, as they call the ex-king of Spain. His green velvet hunting suits, free expenditure of money, conciliating manner and his bullet-proof sleeping chamber are fruitful topics for conversation. The Count de Surveillers spent four summers on his American estate. He was accompanied by a retinue of followers and had as his guests many distinguished French generals, exiles like himself. Their banquets served on golden dishes, were characterized by all the pomp and precision of court etiquette. Some of these noble guests became colonists for a time. Among them were Count Real, who was Napoleon's chief prefect of police, the Duc de Vincennes, a philosopher of eminence; M. Pigeon, an astronomer who brought some of the finest instruments known to the age, to Cape Vincent; Marshal Grouchy, to whose too implicit obedience of orders historians attribute the defeat at Waterloo, and other Napoleonic adherents who joined in building a house for the emperor's occupation when he should escape from St. Helena.

Another member of the Bonaparte family, Napoleon Louis Lucien Murat, likewise became a resident of Jefferson county. He was a son of the brilliant General Murat, Napoleon's greatest cavalry officer (whom he made king of the two Sicilies) and of Caroline, sister of the first consul. The son remained, for a while after Waterloo, with his mother in Spain, until the Bourbons made his residence there too uncomfortable. He then joined the contingent of refugees and bought a tract of land on Indian river near Theresa, where he opened a store, built saw mills and grist mills, and fancied he had founded a city, which he called Joachim in honor of his father. He was a gay and volatile young fellow, and though the fortunes of his family and of his country were, at that time, grave enough to fill a thoughtful mind with apprehensions, he seemed intent upon making life a holiday. His store, instead of being stocked with corduroy and jeans, which were needed by the settlers, was decked out with artificial flowers and French millinery, and at his fantastic entertainments metamorphosed the farmers' daughters, the only young women in the neighborhood, into Cinderellas clothed with delicate silks which he imported and distributed freely among the maids of the Dutch settlement. Among the luxuries which the young prince brought from France was a grand piano, which was preserved only to be burned in the very disastrous fire which visited the village of Carthage in 1881. Its antique pattern showed the legs connected at either end by an elaborately carved harp and braced by a long bar of solid mahogany, also carved, which united the ends as old fashioned chairs were strengthened by a rung extending across the middle. The piano rested upon carved lions' feet while at each end were drawers for music.

Nothing now remains of Joachim, a city "whose glory

passed away while yet it never was." The name, however, still clings to a bridge and dam which were built when the city was planned.

The prince married an American woman who, when their last shred of fortune had vanished, opened a boarding school under the untitled name of Madam Murat. The writer of a sensational article which appeared in Putnam's Magazine in 1853 under the caption "Have We a Bourbon Among us?" attempted to foist upon the world a marvelous tale stating that the well beloved preacher to the Indians, the Rev. Eleazur Williams, was, in reality, the young dauphin son of Louis XVI and Marie Antoinette and that M. Le Ray de Chaumont was the agent of his rescue, escape and preservation in the safe solitudes of Northern New York. M. Vincent Le Ray indignantly denied the charge and gave the denial all the publicity that print and painstaking distribution could provide. Lamartine states that the miracle of silence over his escape would be greater than his miraculous escape itself.

It is to be regretted that a name so worthy of remembrance as is that of Le Ray should be omitted from the pages of history. In a life of Dr. Franklin, which has been recently published, the story of M. Le Ray's hospitality to him is pleasantly told; there also appears a picture of the senior Le Ray and a picture of the house occupied by Dr. Franklin during his nine years' residence in France. The building is still pointed out to tourists as the Franklin house.

M. Le Ray and his family left America and returned to France in June, 1836. He died in December, 1840, aged 80 years, leaving three children and two sisters. Alexander, his youngest son, fell in a duel in Texas in 1844. Theresa, Countess de Gouvello, died in 1853, leaving one son who came to this country in 1881, having been invited by this government to represent the Le Ray family at the centennial celebration of the surrender of Cornwallis at Yorktown. Before returning he visited the old home in Jefferson county. Vincent Le Ray, who succeeded to his father's estate in 1825, was a methodical business man, and though strictly honorable, he possessed none of the liberal qualities of his father. He died in 1886, leaving one son, Charles, Marques de St. Paul, a childless man with whose death the historic name will probably cease.

Two Old-Fashioned Boys.

Ben and Joby Collins were coasting one Saturday half-holiday on a sled with bent runners. Ben was the elder and the more serious. Joby was more athletic, quicker of perception, and slow to believe what he could not see with his own eyes and instantly comprehend. What Ben lacked in the perceptive organs he fully made up in the reflective. Consequently he was slow, in fact, clumsy, and Joby was constantly getting the "start" of him in their boyish divertisements. Ben's easy temperament was the means of avoiding friction over Joby's little victories. They usually agreed except upon scientific matters in which Ben, having a thirst for knowledge, was greatly interested. His rehash of natural philosophy was wholly lost upon Joby who was skeptical and at times bored by his brother's discussion of theoretical and applied science which he found in an old volume borrowed from a neighbor who once lived in Boston.

"Let's take one more slide and then go home, do the chores and get ready for the show," suggested Ben, who, though slow, was really the leading spirit in the enterprises of the Boy's Own Kingdom.

" What is the show, Ben," inquired the other.

"Why, the tallygraph! The thing that talks over twenty miles of wire. The showmen come to paw for to get the schoolhouse to give the show in."

"That's nawthin," answered Joby, its just as easy to talk over a coil of wire as over a handsled. Get on—its my steer."

"But the wire is stretched away miles and miles on poles and they talk to another feller at the other——"

Further explanation was precluded by the speed of the sled down the long slope which dropped them gently on the ice which covered La Famine and the lake as far as the eye could reach.

"Now, once more and I'll steer," urged Ben when they had shot far out on the ice.

They returned to the top of the hill and made a fresh start, Ben lying down and making a rudder of a new copper-toed boot. The course made a sharp turn through an open gate flanked by a rail fence.

Ben steered too much and the sled began to waver in its course.

Look out!" warned Job, and then flung himself off into the snow whither he emerged half suffocated to find the sled high and dry in the rail fence and poor Ben screeching with pain. It was characteristic of Ben's lack of skill that he should slam into the fence.

"Oh! my leg, my leg! It's broke, Joby. Draw me home on the sled. I—feel—so—sick."

Joby was frightened, but as he did things without ever thinking he very quickly mended the wrecked sled with cord and then all but finished Ben in rolling him onto it. He drew his injured brother to the house and made such a hullabaloo for help that his affrighted parents ran to meet him and assist the suffering boy to a trundle bed which was hauled from under the bed in the recess.

A neighbor was sent on horseback for a doctor, sixteen miles distant, and grandmother put a bunch of pennyroyal steeping because as she said "if a sweat did him no good it would do no harm," albeit the victim of the accident was in such pain as to cause the perspiration to moisten his whole body.

The doctor arrived the next day and found the limb already set and bound in splints of bark, a very creditable job, he called it, and left instructions for poor Ben to keep the bed for three weeks, when he would return and examine the limb to determine the success of the process of healing.

Now, be it remembered that the Collins-es were a social people and their home was the resort of neighbors for miles around. Hank Collins was a popular man, though not strong-minded, and while he entertained some political prestige he was not a leader, but a man whose good graces were sought by would-be leaders. Hence his sayings were quoted as from an authority, and he was brought into intercourse with the scattering neighbors more frequently than any other one of them. Moreover he was a subscriber to a weekly paper published in Utica.

Ben always heard what was said by elders in his presence, and pondered much over their discussions which he insisted upon retailing to young Job who did not always exhibit the characteristic of his more patient namesake.

Job went to the schoolhouse in the evening, and for a sixpence saw the new telegraph exhibited. He explained the instrument to Ben in the following not very lucid terms:

"The show didn't mount to nawthink! The feller set up a jigger-jabber on the girls' side and another on our side, and run out some wire along a fence and the trees and brung it back into another winder and hitched it to another jigger. Then he stuck a wire down a knot-hole in the floor, and some more wires into some dishes he called a batter. Then he jiggered one machine and the other jiggered just like it and the two just jigger-jabbered and there wan't nobody anigh to it. He had a paper ribband wound on a wheel and a clock thing run down and made some marks on the ribband just like the marks he made on the blackboard. Then he read the pin scratches on the ribband out loud and said it said 'In God we trust.' I hearn Mr. Marceau say it was all a humbug and we was all fooled. Paw, he says there is somethink in it, but he don't know what. Some say there is and some say he's a vanphilist and made the click-clack on tother jigger with his mouth. You ain't mist anythink and I haint seen anythink. Wusht Ide a saved my sixpence for a hunk of ginger bread next Fourth July." After the recital Job was plied with so many questions that the last were vaguely answered in his sleep. His ideas of the machine were perhaps as clear as those of most of the adults who had been attracted to the exhibition.

Poor Ben! All his life he had wanted to see something and now his pain must be borne with additional grief because deprived of seeing an exhibition of electric science. His feelings upon this subject were not relieved on hearing the discussions of the exhibit which occurred almost daily among the neighbors who called to sympathize with Ben and borrow the newspaper.

During his imprisonment he heard much talk of the election of governor, and Hunkers, Barn Burners, Free Soilers and Mudsills, as well as Anti-Masons. He was well aware that his father was not in sympathy with the latter as he had heard a heated debate between him and Bone Marceau, the latter alleging that he did not want to belong to a party of murderers or have them get into power to secretly kill off their enemies at will and leave the world to wonder who did it.

"But Free Masonry does not encourage that sort of thing any more than does the Church of England," protested Mr. Collins.

"You tell me that! You know as well as I they killed Morgan, threw him into Niagara river and then one night buried him in three graves. You know that hundreds of other unaccountable murders have been committed in the same mysterious way. Do you want a government of murderers?"

"No, I do not. But I do not like to see my—a party called murderers without the proof. A man is innocent until he is proven guilty."

Marceau was a pronounced Anti and no amount of argument would convince him that a Free Mason was not a disguised murderer. So it was agreed that the matter should not be further discussed.

About ten days after this discussion Ben sat upon his trundle-bed, which was far too small, in the house alone. Job, who had become more and more of a companion during Ben's stay in doors, ran in all out of breath.

"Say, Ben, its too durn bad! Can't you walk? Try it. I've just found some of the queerest things in the straw stack. Silver'n gold things!"

Ben's curiosity was fully aroused, besides he had been shut up ten days and was like a caged bird once free.

"I bleeve I can hobble out there and back before anybody comes. I just hopped to the door and back just to see if I could move."

"In course you can," vouched the excited Job. "Ten days is time enough to heal a horse's leg. Here, take gramp's cane and the tongs. I'll help."

Slowly and in fear Ben started on the short journey and with Job's encouragement he reached the stack much to his surprise without any special suffering. Once there Job began throwing the straw, which had been thrashed with a flail, aside with a fork made of the crotch of a hickory stick.

"What's this?" holding up a pair of crossed quills. "And here is a cooper's compass stuck on a square and look at these great keys! Here's pole hooks and a big letter G, and a Bible—would a thief steal a Bible, Ben?"

"Well how do you know any of it's stole," inquired Ben.

"How else could it get into the straw, then," queried Job in turn.

"Well, I don't say as how it was stole, but I just believe its a Free Mason's———"

Job dropped the keys with an exclamation of horror.

"Do you suppose this is what they kill folks with?"

Ben wasn't sure, but at his suggestion the discovery was again secreted in the straw and the boys returned to the house in alarm lest they should meet the fate of Morgan before the return of their parents. And Ben began to feel that perhaps he might suffer great injury from deserting his bed before he had permission.

When the parents returned the boys related the news of their wonderful find to their mother, and she in turn told their father. He seemed surprised and a little frustrated, then sternly bade them not to say a word to a soul about the matter.

Next forenoon Job plucked up courage enough to again remove the straw so as to get another look at the strange

"GO IN JUST ONCE MORE."

objects. He threw out a great lot of the straw and declared he didn't suppose he had buried it so deep. After an extra effort he came down to solid straw which had not been disturbed. Not until then did it occur to him that the wonderful things he had seen and handled had gone just as mysteriously as they had appeared. When he made report of the equally strange disappearance to his father, that worthy laconically dismissed the subject with an imperative:

"Shut up!"

It was but a few days after Job's discovery that the doctor, with mysterious saddle bags, returned to visit his patient, only to find him knocking about with his injured limb lashed to a barrel stave, the convex surface fitting under the knee very comfortably. To the neighbors the boy's leaving his bed a week before the date fixed by the doctor was a triumph of their inherent opposition to professional science.

"But what could you expect," remarked Ben's mother, "what could you expect from a doctor who has a mustache?"

It was agreed that a man so dandified as to grow a mustache could not be very smart to say nothing of professional knowledge. As for Ben, he was too anxious to get away to his accustomed outdoor pastimes to debate the question of the knitting of the bones between the doctor's skill and the awful doses of jalap, boneset tea and calomel administered by his anxious grandmother who had a Thomsonian specific in every weed in the forest.

"I'm just death on the fever," she would say, "and gin me a plenty of fever-weed and pennyroyal, and keep them from a filling themselves with water and I'll warn you they'll come out all right unless it happens as it did with Huldy Dobbins, she that was a Purse. She was outen her head and once when she didn't know what she was about and the watchers was asleep she just went to the spring and drank and drank. I took care of her myself arter that and she was right sick for a fortnight, but she didn't get another drop of water you may depend."

The old lady drew a clay pipe from the ashes where it had been placed to burn it out, and filling it smoked complacently in silence. Ah! Could a machine for recording thought be had what a world of reminiscence could have been rescued from oblivion as the dear old lady smoked and dreamed of her days of activity "down at old Glosster."

Some hardships befell the early settlers on this fertile point, and among the most annoying little things was losing the fire. Mrs. Collins was attending a sick neighbor; her husband had gone to the Harbor with a grist drawn by a yoke of oxen and the trip would require two days. The boys and their grandmother were left alone and such a bustling preparation for dinner had not stirred up the but-and-ben of a house since last Thanksgiving, when the occasion was made memorable by the rescue of four half-drowned settlers who had been cast upon the shore in the night and brought back to life in the hospitable cheer of the Collins fireplace.

The old lady was intent upon getting up a bounteous meal of rye-and-Indian bread and corned beef with cabbage. When she had broiled some salt pork before the embers, and freshened it by dipping the sizzling piece in a gourd of cold water often, and then again bringing it to the coals, she set about further preparation so interestedly as to forget the low fire. When she hung a kettle on the crane she was surprised to find the fire out. Not a live ember remained. There was no tinder box, and the punk Mr. Collins had taken with him.

"Joby," she said solemnly, "the fire's lost. You will have to go down to Uncle Hiram's and get some fire, and get back quick as ever you can. Here, take the tongs, and hurry."

It was two miles to the neighbor's and a four mile trudge in the snow did not promise any unusual amusement. However, he was accustomed to obeying, and that at once. Off he trudged with the tongs astride his neck and in due time made his errand known at the neighbor's door. He walked in without rapping, and was cordially received. A big twisted doughnut and a yellow mug of soup was brought, and the same relished with the truly enviable appetite of a hungry boy.

The end of a burning stick was caught in the tongs and Joby started for home, giving the ember an occasional whirl over his head to keep it "alive." Weary and wet the plucky lad arrived at his father's clearing and climbed the rail and brush fence. His foot slipped and he plunged off into the snow whither he emerged half suffocated. The ember had fallen to the opposite side of the fence and sizzled and smoked and steamed as poor Joby scrambled around in the snow vainly searching for the tongs. These were found lodged in the fence just as he was ready to give up and cry. But his joy was quickly gone. An ominous silence in the neighborhood of the erstwhile sputtering ember filled him with disappointment. The cherished live coal was black and dead.

Job let out just one wail, and then resolutely turned back for another brand, and in so doing exhibited the courage and fortitude of the pioneers who subdued the wooded and rocky Black River country. Our young hero was successful in the second effort, and as he dried himself before the big crackling fire he soon recovered his wonted spirits and animation.

His father returned unexpectedly that night having left the grist to be ground next day, and it was agreed that Mr.

Marceau should remain with the grist. What was his surprise on going after it to meet Mr. Marceau who had returned five or six miles of the distance and brought the two bags of grist by carrying one some distance and setting it down, returning for the other. He was careful not to get either out of his sight, and in the return traversed the distance three times.

Spring arrived with its attendant floods and a big run of suckers, which created no end of amusement for the few boys in the neighborhood who had a great joke on Bone Marceau. He and another neighbor were catching suckers with a small scoopnet, and the better to preserve them they were thrown in a rockhole which contained water. They had captured almost a hundred of them when they decided that it were needless to continue the slaughter. They were not a little surprised to find not a fish in the hole and still more surprised to find in it a communication with the creek out of which the one poor sucker passed and repassed only to be caught up and tossed back again until almost exhausted. Joking Marceau was a serious thing, however, especially as Tubbs, the cooper, had related the incident and the boys knew him for a funny old joker.

Tubbs was a prime favorite with the boys. He had told them that he was in a circus before his arrival in their community and the wonderful feats he performed and saw performed completely won the boys over to holding a candle for him as he worked of an evening, and to go on all manner of errands. He told them the most delightful bogie stories about banshees and death-ticks.

A favorite yarn was his experience of driving a corpse at a funeral "down east." He had a pair of horses attached to a long sled.

"The ground was bare in spots" said he, "and rough in places. The coffin was placed in the sled and all went well until the descent of a big hill was commenced. It was bare and rough. The coffin jolted around a good deal and bimby the lid rattled off. The corpse was a man who had long whiskers under his chin. I glanced backward over my shoulder and got a fair look at him. His whiskers were blowing over the edge of the coffin and as I was at the lower end of the sled I thought he was getting up to take me. I put the birch on the horses and broke away from the perseshun and brought up at the graveyard half an hour ahead of the others. But it was mighty queer the lid had got back to its place and I always bleeved the old feller just reached out for it and fastened himself in."

Just then old Jimmy came back from the woods whither he had been sent by the cooper to fetch the horse. Jimmy was a wit and he and the cooper were never happier than when bandying each other with a half dozen boys to appreciate their sayings. Jimmy stuttered badly at times and on this occasion he returned without the horse.

"S-s-t-d-d-ggg" stammered poor Jimmy.

"Sing it," shouted the cooper.

"The divil a harse cud I see-e!" sang Jimmy, and the boys dodged behind the shop to have a laugh at the unexpected response.

It was April and the Collins boys and some others had an undivided interest in a log canoe. With such a frail craft they made long excursions up and down shore, and even rigged up a square sail out of a woolen blanket. They sailed to the islands and paddled back, proud of their skill as navigators, and even talked of a voyage to the Harbor to see the general training. But it was soon swimming time and they lived a life worth living.

The first swim of the season chilled them blue but they

declared the water warm and on coming out met Valiant Smith and he, holding up two fingers and proposed they go in again.

"Go in just once more," he plead, and although quaking the boys all plunged back and never a one was the worse for the cold dip.

SCHOOL

The summer term of the district school was to open with a lady teacher. The building was made of squared logs and warmed with a big fireplace opposite the only door. Pine seats ran around the walls, and these were confronted by pine desks attached to which was a low seat which served the purpose of recitation seats.

During the preceding winter term a blackboard had been placed on either side of the door. A water pail occupied a bench on the right and a high desk filled the portion of the opposite side not occupied by the seats. Paper wads crusted the ceiling, and the seats showed strange characters deep-carved and filled with dried ink. The windows were small and filled with "seven-by-nine" panes. The "forest primeval" grew in the yard, and primitive rocks, rearing their ugly heads out of the soil, stubbed many a bare toe the while the term lasted.

Ben and Job arose early on the first day of school and just at daylight repaired to the schoolhouse, and crawling into a window, selected their seats for the term. Others soon arrived and as they worked their way in Ben and Job set up a yell that scared the intruders almost into fits. Their seats selected and books deposited, an adjournment was taken to the yard, some bats and a leather-covered ball were produced and a game of four-old-cat was started. Ben was catcher, and he got too close to the bat. As the batsman, with a foot on the bye, drew back to sock the ball out into the woods his club came in contact with Ben's face. The smile faded and tears flowed.

"I just wanted to see if I could strike the ball hard enough to make the fire fly as Tubbs says he usto," said the striker, "but I didn't know Ben was so close."

The repairs took some time and when the boys were ready for something else the teacher arrived. She was a little woman of uncertain age, but full of determination. The boys hung about the door while the big barefooted girls went spat, spat into the schoolhouse behind the teacher. Soon there was a cloud of dust issuing from the door and windows.

"Will some of the young gentlemen bring in some cedar boughs for the fire-place?"

Slowly they started. "Young gentlemen," they repeated, but all the same they brought in more than would fill the black cavern of a fireplace. A sharp rapping on the window assembled the school in their seats and the reign of the new teacher was fairly begun over a colony of homespun trowsers and gingham aprons.

The first class in reading was called out and stood in a row in front of the teacher's desk. The book used was the English Reader which was filled with horrible narratives of Indian massacre, sufferings of wrecked humanity at sea, earthquakes, executions and death in frightful form. On the other hand the work contains some of the best selections of English verse as well as prose in existence. To test the new comers in the class the following selections were read from books with wooden covers:

Come where th' industrious bees had stor'd,
In artful cells, their luscious hoard ;
O'erjoy'd they seized, with eager haste,
Luxurious on the rich repast.
Alarm'd at this, the little crew
About their ears vindictive flew.

The beasts, unable to sustain
Th' unequal combat, quit the plain ;
Half-blind with rage, and mad with pain,
Their native shelter they regain ;
There sit, and now, discreeter grown,
Too late their rashness they bemoan ;
And this by dear experience gain,
That pleasure's ever bought with pain.

So when the gilded baits of vice
Are plac'd before our longing eyes,
With greedy haste we snatch our fill,
And swallow down the latent ill ;
But when experience opens our eyes,
Away the fancied pleasure flies,
It flies, but oh ! too late we find,
It leaves a real sting behind.

THE YOUTH AND THE PHILOSOPHER.

A Grecian youth of talents rare,
Whom Plato's philosophic care
Had form'd for virtue's nobler view,
By precept and example too,
Would often boast his matchless skill,
To curb the steed and guide the wheel ;
And as he pass'd the gazing throng,

TWO OLD-FASHIONED BOYS.

With graceful ease, and smack'd the thong.
The idiot wonder they express'd,
Was praise and transport to his breast.

At length, quite vain, he needs would show
His master what his art could do,
And bade his slaves the chariot lead
To Academus' sacred shade.
The trembling grove confess'd its fright,
The wood-nymphs started at the sight:
The muses drop the learned lyre,
And to their inmost shades retire.

Howe'er, the youth, with forward air,
Bows to the sage, and mounts the car.
The lash resounds, the coursers spring,
The chariot marks the rolling ring.
And gath'ring crowds, with eager eyes,
And shouts, pursue him as he flies.

Triumphant to the goal return'd,
With nobler thirst his bosom burn'd ;
And now along th' idented plain,
The self-same track he marks again,
Pursues with care the nice design,
Nor ever deviates from the line.
Amazement seiz'd the circling crowd :
The youths with emulation glow'd ;
Ev'n bearded sages hail'd the boy ;
And all but Plato gaz'd with joy.

For he, deep-judging sage, beheld
With pain the triumphs of the field ;
And when the charioteer drew nigh,

And, flush'd with hope, had caught his eye—
"Alas! unhappy youth," he cry'd,
"Expect no praise from me," (and sigh'd.)
" With indignation I survey
Such skill and judgment thrown away ;
The time profusely squander'd there,
On vulgar arts beneath thy care,
If well employ'd, at less expense,
Had taught thee honor, virtue, sense ;
And rais'd thee from a coachman's fate,
To govern men, and guide the state."

EARTHQUAKE AT CATANEA.

One of the earthquakes most particularly described in story is that which happened in the year 1693; the damages which were chiefly felt in Sicily, but its motion was perived in Germany, France and England. It extended to a rcumference of two thousand six hundred leagues, chiefly fecting the sea coasts and great rivers, more perceivable also on the mountains than in the valleys.

Its motions were so rapid that persons who lay at their ngth, were tossed from side to side as upon a rolling billow. ie walls were dashed from their foundations, and no fewer an fifty cities, with an increditable number of villages, were ther destroyed or greatly damaged. The city of Catanea in rticular was utterly overthrown. A traveller who was on his iy thither perceived at the distance of some miles, a black oud like night, hanging over the place.

The sea all of a sudden began to roar, Mount Ætna to nd forth great spires of flames, and soon after a shock ended with a noise as if all the artillery in the world had been once discharged. Our traveller being obliged to alight instantly, felt himself raised a foot from the ground, and turning his eyes to the city he with amazement saw nothing but a thick cloud of dust in the air.

The birds flew about astonished, the sun was darkened, the beasts ran howling from the hills, and although the shock did not continue above three minutes, yet near nineteen thousand of the inhabitants of Sicily, perished in the ruins. Catanea, to which city the describer was traveling, seemed the principal scene of ruin, its place only was to be found, and not a footstep of its former magnificence was to be seen remaining.

The following lines were read in concert, and thundering accent of the boys with changing voices which sometimes rose to a strange falsetto, mingled with the piping sopranos was indeed a strange exhibition of rhetorical exercises:

THE NIGHTINGALE AND THE GLOW-WORM.

A nightingale, that all day long
Had cheer'd the village with his song,
Nor yet at eve his note suspended,
Nor yet when eventide was ended,
Began to feel, as well he might,
The keen demands of appetite;
When, looking eagerly around,
He spied far off upon the ground,
A something shining in the dark,
And knew the glow-worm by his spark.
So, stooping down from hawthorn top
He thought to put him in his crop.

The worm, aware of his intent,
Harangued him thus, right eloquent—

"Did you admire my lamp," quoth he,
"As much as I your minstrelsy,
You would abhor to do me wrong,
As much as I to spoil your song;
For 'twas the self-same pow'r divine,
Taught you to sing and me to shine;
That you with music, I with light,
Might beautify and cheer the night."

The songster heard his short oration,
And, warbling out his approbation,
Releas'd him, as my story tells,
And found a supper somewhere else.
Hence, jarring sectaries may learn,
Their real int'rest to discern;
That brother should not war with brother
And worry and devour each other:
But sing and shine by sweet consent,
Till life's poor, transient night is spent;
Respecting in each other's case
The gifts of nature and of grace.

Those Christians best deserve the name,
Who studiously make peace their aim:
Peace, both the duty and the prize
Of him that creeps, and him that flies.

The teacher wishing to introduce a new reader placed in ands of her pupils a new book called the American Pre- r, and to instruct the class they were permitted to read r than was the custom. And the following selections " practiced " upon:

SINGULAR ADVENTURE OF GENERAL PUTNAM.

When General Putnam first moved to Pomfret, in Connecticut, in the year 1739, the country was new and much infested with wolves. Great havoc was made among the sheep by a she wolf which with her annual whelps, had for several years continued in that vicinity. The young ones were commonly destroyed by the vigilance of the hunters; but the old one was too sagacious to be ensnared by them.

This wolf, at length, became such an intolerable nuisance, that Mr. Putnam entered into a combination with five of his neighbors to hunt alternately until they could destroy her. Two by rotation, were to be constantly in pursuit. It was known, that, having lost the toes from one foot by a steel trap, she made one track shorter than the other.

By this vestige, the pursuers recognized, in a light snow, the route of this pernicious animal. Having followed her to the Connecticut river, and found she had turned back in a direct course towards Pomfret, they immediately returned, and by ten o'clock the next morning the bloodhounds had driven her into a den, about three miles distant from the house of Mr. Putnam.

The people soon collected with dogs, guns, straw, fire and sulphur, to attack the common enemy. With this apparatus, several unsuccessful efforts were made to force her from the den. The hounds came back badly wounded and refused to return. The smoke of blazing straw had no effect. Nor did the fumes of burnt brimstone, with which the cavern was filled, compel her to quit the retirement.

Wearied with such fruitless attempts (which had brought the time to ten o'clock at night) Mr. Putnam tried once more to make his dog enter, but in vain: he proposed to his negro man to go down into the cavern and shoot the wolf. The negro declined the hazardous service.

Then it was that their master, angry at the disappointment, and declaring that he was ashamed of having a coward in his family, resolved himself to destroy the ferocious beast, lest she should escape through some unknown fissure of the rock.

His neighbors strongly remontrated against the perilous enterprise; but he knowing that wild animals were intimidated by fire, and having provided several strips of birch bark, the only conbustible material which he could obtain, which would afford light in this deep and darksome cave, prepared for his descent.

Having accordingly, divested himself of his coat and waistcoat, and having a long rope fastened round his legs, by which he might be pulled back, at a concerted signal, he entered, head foremost, with the blazing torch in his hand.

Having groped his passage till he came to a horizontal part of the den, the most terrifying darkness appeared in front of the dim circle of light afforded by the torch. It was silent as the house of death. None but monsters of the desert had ever before explored this solitary mansion of horror.

He cautiously proceeding onward, came to an ascent, which he slowly mounted on his hands and knees until he discovered the glaring eyeballs of the wolf, who was sitting at the extremity of the cavern. Startled at the sight of fire, she gnashed her teeth and gave a sullen growl.

As soon as he had made the necessary discovery he kicked the rope as a signal for pulling him out. The people, at the mouth of the den, who had listened with painful anxiety, hearing the growling of the wolf, and supposing their friend to be in the most imminent danger, drew him forth with such celerity that he was stripped of his clothes, and severely bruised.

After he had adjusted his clothes, and loaded his gun

with nine buck shot, holding a torch in one hand and the musket in the other, he descended a second time. When he drew nearer than before, the wolf assuming a still more fierce and terrible appearance, howling, rolling her eyes, snapping her teeth, and dropping her head between her legs was evidently in the attitude and on the point of springing on him.

At this critical instant he leveled and fired at her head. Stunned with the shock and suffocated with the smoke he immediately found himself drawn out of the cave. But having refreshed himself and permitted the smoke to dissipate he went down a third time.

Once more he came within sight of the wolf, who appearing very passive, he applied the torch to her nose, and perceiving her dead, he took hold of her ears and then kicking the rope, still tied round his legs, the people above with no small exultation, dragged them both out together.

STORY OF LOGAN, A MINGO CHIEF.

In the spring of the year 1774, a robbery and murder were committed on an inhabitant of the frontiers of Virginia by two Indians of the Shawanese tribe. The neighboring whites, according to their custom, undertook to punish this outrage in a summary way. Colonel Cresap, a man infamous for the many murders he had committed on these much injured people, collected a party and proceeded down the Kanhaway in quest of vengeance.

Unfortunately, a canoe of women and children, with one man only, was seen coming from the opposite shore, unarmed, and unsuspecting any hostile attack from the whites. Cresap and his party concealed themselves on the bank of the river, and the moment the canoe reached th shore, singled out their objects, and, at one fire, killed every person in it.

This happened to be the family of Logan, who had long been distinguished as the friend of the whites. This unworthy return provoked his vengeance. He accordingly signalized himself in the war which ensued.

In the autumn of the same year, a decisive battle was fought at the mouth of the Great Kenhaway, between the collected forces of the Shawanese, Mingoes and Delawares, and a detachment of the Virginia militia. The Indians were defeated and sued for peace.

Logan, however, disdained to be seen among the supplicants; but, lest the sincerity of a treaty should be distrusted, from which so distinguished a chief absented himself, he sent by a messenger, the following speech, to be delivered to Lord Dunmore:

"I appeal to any white man to say if ever he entered Logan's cabin hungry, and he gave him no meat; if ever he came cold and naked, and he clothed him not. During the last long and bloody war, Logan remained idle in his cabin, an advocate for peace.

"Such was my love for the whites, that my countrymen pointed as they passed by, and said, Logan is the friend of white men. I had even thought to have lived with you, had it not been for the injuries of one man. Colonel Cresap, the last spring, in cold blood, and unprovoked, murdered all the relations of Logan, not even sparing my women and children.

"There runs not a drop of my blood in the veins of any living creature. This called on me for revenge. I have fought it; I have killed many; I have fully glutted my vengeance. For my country, I rejoice at the beams of peace; but do not harbor a thought that mine is the joy of fear.

Logan never felt fear. He will not turn on his heel to save his life. Who is there to mourn for Logan? Not one."

This exercise over, the smaller children were called out and read from Webster's spelling book. There was no intermediary reader between the speller and the English reader. Passing upward from the one to the other was a severe test, but one coveted by those who knew by rote the story of the Maid and the Milk, the boy in the apple tree who would not come down when the farmer threw grass, and the other few moral stories "for the instruction of the very young."

Ben often declared that "'rithmetic was his best holt," and it was therefore with a secret delight that he joined the class when it was called. He felt that here was one subject at least in which he would fully acquit himself and make an impression of the acquirement upon the new teacher. The textbook was "Ruger's New System of Arithmetick." The publisher was William Ruger, A. B., author of a grammar and at least one other school-book, and printed in Watertown, N. Y., by Knowlton & Rice.

The inside pages were scrawled over with a quill, and quaint were the sentiments recorded on the fly leaves. Here is one:

Whose tongue ran a great deal too fast for his wit.
He talked of his art and abundance of metal,
So I asked him to make me a flat-bottom kettle.
Let the top and the bottom diameters be
In just such proportion as five is to three;
Twelve inches the depth I proposed and no more,
To hold in ale gallons seven less than a score.
He promised to do it and straight to work went,
But when he had done it he found it too scant.
Thus altering it often too big and too little,
The tinker at last quite spoiled his kettle.
He says he will bring his sad promise to pass,
Or else he will spoil every ounce of his brass.
Now show your skill, you learned youth,
And by your work this sum produce.

Job wrestled like Jacob, but like the tinker his pot was at times too large and anon too small. After giving it up he left this couplet on the board:

The tinker man's problem I've failed to settle.
May Old Nick catch him and his flat-bottom kettle.

Another problem in rhyme was given the class and a merit mark promised the one who should reach the correct answer first. It ran in this wise:

As I was hunting on the forest grounds,
Up starts a hare before my two grey-hounds;
The dogs, being light of foot, did fairly run
Unto her fifteen rods just twenty-one.
The distance that she started up before
Was four score and sixteen rods, just, and no more;
Now this I'd have you unto me declare—
How far they ran before they caught the hare.

Ben applied the good old Rule of Three and obtained the

correct answer long before the others, and having awakened his Muse he expressed the result in the following rhyme:

Old Ruger's hare was raced at unseeming odds,
And lost her life at three hundred thirty-six rods.

The class was examined in vulgar fractions and divided into two classes. The first class was examined in Fellowship and closed with some examples in Tare and Tret. A few paragraphs from the explanatory notes under this head are appended:

Tare and tret are allowances made to the buyer, on the weight of some particular commodities.

Tare is an allowance made for the weight of the barrel, box, bag, or whatever contains the articles or goods.

Tret is an allowance of 4lb. on every 104lb. for waste, dust, etc.

Cloff is an allowance, on some commodities, of 2lb. on every cwt. to turn the scale, or to make the weight hold out, when goods are reweighed, and is claimed chiefly, or only, by the merchants of London.

Scuttle is what remains after a part of the allowance is deducted from the gross weight.

Net weight is what remains after all allowances are made.

The class in arithmetic was dismissed with another poetical problem:

  Friend John, who had in credit liv'd,
  Though now reduc'd, a sum receiv'd—
  This lucky hit 's no sooner found,
  Than clam'rous duns came swarming round:
  To th' landlord—baker—many more.
  John paid, in all, pounds ninety-four.
  Half what remain'd, a friend he lent.
  On Joan and 'self one-fifth he spent;

And when of all these sums bereft,
One-tenth o' th' sum received had left ;
Now show your skill, you learned youths,
And by your work the sum produce.

"Recess!" said the teacher. Pell mell the boys in long-tailed coats set off with big brass buttons and the girls in pantalettes rushed out and raced themselves red playing hi-spy, pom-pom-pullaway and hunt the hare. A smart rapping on the window recalled them again to study. Joby Collins had a scheme which he cherished so closely as to almost fear some of the boys would hear him think. They were not fairly seated when he broke out :

"Teacher! Can Welcome Pettit and me go after a pail of water?"

Yes, they could go, and so carrying the bucket between them they trudged away rejoicing at cutting the hours of study just so much short. When they returned the infant class was studying the alphabet in the spelling book. Then the second class in spelling was called out. The system of leaving off at the head every night was in vogue, and mighty were the strifes for that coveted honor. Job and his companion joined the class after passing the water, a privilege that was too often made the excuse for a poor lesson. Job, as usual, drifted slowly but surely to the foot of the class.

"Drag," pronounced the teacher.

One after another missed the word until it came to Job.

"Now, Joby," said the teacher encouragingly, "you spell drag and you shall go clear to the head."

"Yes, mom," replied Job, and he struck an attitude of deep thought. Suddenly he almost shouted :

"Drag. S–l–r, drag!" And he fairly ran to the head of the class whence the teacher had not the heart to mar the glory of his victory by correcting his orthography, and dismissed the class amid a temporary reign of sensational disorder.

"First class in spelling."

Again the big boys and girls lined up and read a page beginning with these paragraphs:

Let not reading cause you to neglect spelling. Learn to spell and pronounce before you read much.

Good spelling is the sure way to good reading, therefore, study spelling with the greatest care, until you can spell all the words in this book, as soon as you hear them, without seeing them.

When you can spell well, you will soon become a good reader; and as soon as you shall be able to read well, you will be permitted to study grammar.

Grammar will teach you what is meant by the parts of speech, and how to speak and write as you ought; and without the knowledge of grammar, your language will be incorrect, and you will always be marked by your friends as a poor scholar.

Then the good old poem about the rose was read. Some there be who can recite it from memory:

THE ROSE.

How fair is the rose, what a beautiful flower!
In summer so fragrant and gay!
But the leaves are beginning to fade in an hour,
And they wither and die in a day.

Yet the rose has one powerful virtue to boast
Above all the flowers of the field:
When its leaves are all dead, and its fine colors lost,
Still how sweet a perfume it will yield.

So frail are the youth and the beauty of men,
  Though they look gay and bloom like the rose ;
Yet all our fond care to preserve them is vain,
  Time kills them as fast as he goes.
Then I'll not be proud of my youth or my beauty,
  Since both will soon wither and fade ;
But gain a good name by performing my duty ;
  This will scent, like the rose, when I'm dead.

Following the reading the words in the lesson were "put out," words that Ben declared Noah Webster himself could not spell and in fact did not, in some instances, correctly:

Electioneer,	Circumlution,
Proportionable,	Circumvallation,
Confectionary,	Prognostication,
Agglutination,	Transfiguration,
Amalgamation,	Constitutionalist,
Approximation,	Plenipotentiary,
Calumniation,	Excommunication.

Then the class was lead over a rocky territory of words of the same pronunciation, but of different spelling and definition :

Ail, to pain or trouble.
Ale, a kind of beer.
Air, one of the elements.
Ere, before, sooner than.
Heir, an inheritor.
Aisle, the walk in a church.
I'll, contraction for I will.
Ait, a small island in a river.
Ate, the preterit of eat.
Eight, twice four.

Cere, to cover with wax.
Sear, dry ; to burn.
Seer, a prophet.
Sere, withered.
Slaie, a weaver's reed.
Sleigh, a kind of carriage.
Slay, to kill.
Sley, to part into threads.
Permiscible, that which may be mingled.
Permissible, that which may be permitted.
Aother piece of poetry was read with strong accents by the teacher and deserves a place in the storehouse of memory:

WHAT IS CHARITY?

'Tis not to pause when at my door
  A shivering brother stands ;
To ask the cause that made him poor,
  Or why he help demands.

'Tis not to spurn that brother's prayer
  For faults he once has known ;
'Tis not to leave him in despair,
  And say that I have none.

The voice of charity is kind—
  She thinketh nothing wrong ;
To every fault she seemeth blind,
  Nor vaunteth with her tongue.

In penitence she placeth faith—
  Hope smileth at her door ·
Relieveth first—Then softly saith,
  " Go, brother, sin no more."

The class numbered and retired to their seats whence

they were soon hurrying out for noon. The afternoon program was varied with the substitution of geography for the arithmetic. It contained no illustrations, no maps and was a dull, tedious study. The work was accompanied by an atlas to which reference was seldom had. It was the work of Daniel Adams, A. M., author of the arithmetic. The lessons begin with

THE WORLD.

The world or earth is a large globe, the diameter of which is nearly eight thousand miles, and its surface contains nearly 200 millions of square miles.

It is 96 millions of miles from the sun, about which it revolves once a year; and turns round on its own axis every day.

The earth is generally divided into four unequal parts, called quarters; Europe, Asia, Africa, and America.

Eorope is the smallest division, but is distinguished for its learning, politeness, government, and laws; for the industry of its inhabitants, and the temperature of its climate. It is the only quarter of the globe which has yet been fully explored and known.

In Asia, the human race was first planted, and there the most remarkable transactions occurred, which are recorded in the scripture history.

Africa has been always in a state of barbarism, if we except the Egyptians, those ancient fathers of learning, and Carthage, once the rival of the Roman Empire.

America was unknown to the inhabitants of the other continent, till a little more than three hundred years ago, when it was discovered by Christopher Columbus; and hence it is frequently called the New World, in contradiction to the

Eastern continent, first known, and hence called the Old World.

The descriptive geography was unique. In a chapter on the lakes it says:

Lake Erie is noted for having its islands and banks, at the west end, so infested with rattle-snakes as to render it dangerous to land on them. Near the banks of the islands it is covered with the large pond lily, the leaves of which lie on the surface of the water so thick as to cover it entirely for many acres together; on these in the summer seasons lie myraids of water-snakes, basking in the sun. On this lake, the American fleet, under Com. Perry, Sept. 10, 1813, gained over the British fleet of larger force, a splendid and important victory.

EARTHQUAKES.

There are numerous proofs that earthquakes have been violent in various parts of America. Nearly fifty have been noticed in the New England States, since the settlement of the first English colony at Plymouth, in 1620. Of these, five have been particularly memorable, viz. 1638, 1658, 1663, 1727, 1755, as being much heavier than the rest. They have all commenced with an undulatory motion, in a direction from north-west to south-east, the central course of which, or place of greatest violence, has been in a line coinciding nearly with lake Ontario and the mouth of Merrimack river, extending southward to the Potomac, and northward to the St. Lawrence. The whole country within these limits has been repeatedly shaken, most violently about the middle, and least towards the south-west and north-east boundaries. In those five, before mentioned as being particularly memorable, the violence of the shocks was such as to cause the bells in churches to ring; many chimnies were thrown down, and in some instances houses ; furniture dropped from the shelves on which it stood; the earth in many places was rent, and quantities of sand thrown out, of a highly sulphurous smell. Some remarkable alterations were observed in wells and springs of water about the time of these earthquakes. In some, the quality of the water was altered ; in others, the quantity. New springs were opened, and old ones dried up.

FISHERIES.

The greatest part of the fisheries of the United States is carried on by the citizens of Massachusetts. The people of Nantucket, New Bedford and Cape Cod, carry on the whale fishery. These fish, however, at present, are rare about the Cape, although formerly caught there in great numbers. A species of the whale kind, called black fish, weighing about 5 tons, and affording oil, is very abundant. The manner of catching them is very singular. They swim in shoals of several hundreds, and the inhabitants put off in their boats and drive them ashore, like so many cattle, on the flats, where they are left by the tide, and fall an easy prey.

WASHINGTON.

The city of Washington, situated on the Maryland side of the Potowmack, is the seat of government of the United States. It is laid out on a plan, which, if completed, will render it one of the handsomest and most commodious cities in the world. The streets north and south are crossed by others at right angles ; these are transversely crossed by 15 other streets named after the different states. The houses are mostly of brick. The capitol, when completed, will present a front of 362 feet. It is pleasantly situated on an eminence, commanding a view of every part of the city, and of a considerable portion of the country around. The president's house is 170 by 85 feet, two stories high, of free, white stone. It stands on a rising ground, possessing a water prospect, together with a view of the capitol, and of the most material parts of the city. The population in 1810 was 8,208.

MICHIGAN TERRITORY.

Detroit is the capital. The old town was wholly destroyed by fire in 1805. The new town is well laid out; the streets cross each other at right angles. It is a place of considerable trade, which consists chiefly in a barter of coarse European goods with the natives for furs. The town is surrounded by a strong blockade, through which there are four gates. On the west side there is a small fort. The streets are generally crowded with Indians in the day time; but at night they are all shut out of the town, except such as get admittance into private houses, and the gates are closed.

The school was closed with writing, spelling and the announcement that some of scholars were far enough advanced to begin the study of grammar as soon as books could be procured, and thus on the first day did the little teacher arouse an unusual interest in the little kingdom over which she was to reign supreme for four months at $2.00 per week and "board around."

When the Collins boys returned home from school they found some neighbors present and considerable excitement was manifested. There were two events, one domestic and the public, either sufficient to throw a family or a nation into excitement. To the boys the advent of a stove was a marvel. Considering his wife's exposure to the heat of a fire-place during the summer, Mr. Collins had purchased the first stove ever seen in the community and a happier woman than their mother did not live, notwithstanding she had some misgivings over becoming familiar with its mechanism.

"I will try it first on some wheat flour biscuits, and if it bakes we will have some for the preacher when he comes the Sunday after next," said the good woman with a merited touch of pride.

Job and Ben agreed it would be fun to work up wood for the little thing, and then gave their attention to their father who was reading from the Bedford Intelligencer the news of an outbreak at Niagara. The account is here given verbatim:

We hasten to lay before our readers, in an extra, the latest intelligence, from the contending armies on the Niagara frontier, received here last evening in the Cleveland daily Herald and Gazette of January 2d. The accounts are from the Buffalo papers, and will be read with much interest.

The patriots were still, at our last accounts, December 30th, strongly intrenched on Navy island, which is a small British island, two miles above the Niagara falls, and is partly covered from view from the American shore by the lower end of Grand Island, which belongs to the United States.

The British royalists had made several attempts on the island, but were as often repulsed by the patriots. And reports at Buffalo were that the royal forces and Indians had landed and taken possession of Grand island, which news created a great ferment at Buffalo. The excitement there was great on the 29th, but on the 30th, the news of the capture and burning, and sending over the great cataract of the American steamboat Caroline, found lying at the American village of Slosser, opposite Chippewa, with all on board but twelve, may be expected to have heightened the excitement to its highest pitch.

This is our latest news, and its effect at Buffalo when communicated there, we can well imagine.

Indeed the Herald informs us that the excitement was intense in Buffalo on Saturday and a brigade of militia was ordered out to rendezvous in that city and part of the 208th regiment was ordered on duty on Saturday evening.

A meeting was held in Cleveland, Jan. 1st, at which resolutions were passed expressing their sympathy with the Canadian patriots and with our own citizens who are exposed to tory outrage and violence. J. R. St. John and Samuel Cook presided at the meeting, and a committee of 21 gentlemen was appointed to receive donations for the benefit of the patriots.

General Southerland, from the patriot camp at Navy Island, was present and addressed the meeting and was loudly cheered.

Report says that a company of sixty volunteers left Cleveland yesterday in a steamboat for Navy Island.

The sheriff immediately dispatched an express, who was accompanied by two of the United States marshals recently appointed, to ascertain if a landing by the British troops had actually taken place, preparatory to his making a call on the county militia to enforce their expulsion. These particulars were explained to the multitude assembled in the street by W. H. Eagers, Esq., district attorney, who stated in his remarks, that the necessary legal measures would be taken, and on the return of the express, if it was found necessary to claim the aid of our militia to enforce them, due notice would be given.

Four o'clock P. M.: The express has just returned and reports that a small band of British Indians had landed on Grand island, and a large boat load of the royalists attempted to reach the same spot this morning, but were forced to return to the Canada shore with the loss of six killed.

We give the above statement of the course pursued by our citizens as a precaution to the people abroad, from believing the many and erroneous reports which reach them, coming as they do, magnified and distorted in every possible shape.

From one of the officers of the patriot army who arrived in town this evening, we have received a verbal account of the attempt last night by the royalists to make the descent on Navy island. Early on yesterday morning the royalists commenced the erection of a battery with six embrasures on the Canada shore for the ostensible purpose of raking the southwest corner of the island, and under cover of their guns allow inganother party to make a descent from a point about half a mile above. As soon as their operations were discovered, the patriots commenced a fire from ten guns, the shot nearly destroying the works of the enemy and causing men and officers to abandon them. Previous to this, however, a continued fire had been kept up from Chippewa to the highest point above, which was not returned by the islanders.

Everything remained quiet until late in the afternoon, no persons to be seen on the Canadian side but a few sentinels, when the alarm was given that a number of boats had put out from Chippewa creek to make an attack. The artillery immediately opened upon them, destroying one or two of the barges and forcing them to drop back with the current. A company of infantry also fired several volleys with effect, the number killed not ascertained.

About 11 o'clock at night, the royalists pushed over from the point above, running under the shore of Grand Island in this state, but put back after they were convinced by the signals on Grand Island and a few shots, that they were discovered.

They then commenced again to build their breastworks but were driven out. This morning at day break another attempt met the like result. McNab and his men have now retired upon Chippewa.

From the Buffalo Commercial, Dec. 29, 2 o'clock p. m. Gov. Head arrived at Chippewa yesterday, with four hundred volunteers from Cobourg, brought in two steamboats from Toronto.

The cannonading heard early this morning destroyed the royalists' hydra-head brest-works again, which seem to spring up every night, merely to be cut down in the morning. Between 60 and 70 guns were fired to accomplish their destruction.

A boat was discovered near the head of Grand island early this morning, which was fired upon and several supposed to have been killed or wounded, as those in it were observed to carry some of their numbers on shore on reaching the Canadian side. It probably contained a reconnoitering party.

The redoubtable Col. Sutherland, alias Duke of Lancaster, has been sent with dispatches to Dr. Duncomb in the western part of the province.

Our express met loads of individuals, armed and unarmed, together with footmen and horsemen, perhaps sixty or seventy in all, bound post haste for the scene of action.

Volunteers seem to be pouring in from all quarters. Rochester furnishes a full quota.

From the Buffalo Commercial, Dec. 30. The following was issued this morning, as an extra, from this office:

Capt. Keeler, of the schooner Agnes Barton, and F. Emmons, of this city, have just brought news by express from Slosser, of an attack made this morning upon the steamboat Caroline, lying at that place, which resulted in the destruction of the boat, and the death of twenty-two of her crew, only 12 escaped.

It is stated that the attack was made about 2 o'clock, by five boats of armed loyalists, containing from 100 to 150 men who guarded the gangways, and cried " no quarters!"

Capt. Appleby, of the Constitution, who went down as pilot of the Caroline yesterday, narrowly escaped with his life. He received a flesh wound, and was pursued to the house adjoining.—A Mr. Durfer, lately belonging to the Stage office at the Eagle, in this city, lies on the dock with his brains blown out.

The Caroline was then set on fire, and finally drifted out into the current, and went over the falls.

We give the above, just as it was received, without vouching for any of the particulars. It may be proper to add, that Captain Keeler, as we are informed, saw the result of the scene above described.

The twelve o'clock express confirms the news of this morning, It is said that the Caroline was filled with visitors and not soldiers. The word with the loyalists was, " No prisoners!—no quarters!" Those who attempted to escape were killed, with a few exceptions—the boat was set on fire, and with the remainder towed into the current on the Canadian side, which soon carried her over the falls. The loyalists gave three cheers for Victoria, and under cover of the darkness, it is supposed escaped the fire opened upon them from the island. Those on the boat slept there, because the public houses were full.

Captain Harding, of the brig Indiana, escaped with a

severe wound in the head; only one man was found on the shore, the one above mentioned, the rest reported missing—there is little doubt but they went over the falls with the burning steamboat.

This piece of "news" reached the settlement four months after it was printed, and it did not reach the Intelligencer office until a week after its occurrence. Sympathy for the Canadian patriots was expressed in the neighborhood and a few secret lodges were organized and a rendezvous had on the St. Lawrence. Some few enlisted in the foolish cause, and some lost their lives in the "Battle of the Windmill," others were executed at Kingston, and still others banished to Van Dieman's land.

These events did in no wise interfere with the school, which had now really entered upon a new era in the matter of learning. For a wonder the blue beech gads were not once used, and the teaching of manners went hand in hand with grammar. The boys removed their hats when greeting their elders, and the girls courtesied.

Joby set sail on an unknown sea one noon, when, with an innate love of mischief, some of his companions had removed and eaten every scrap of the lunch in his basket, and then filled it with grass.

"It's just too mean, Joby, and you shall have half of mine," said Nancy Marceau. Job felt meaner than ever, but he somehow just couldn't refuse. That night he carried her books, and as her home was reached he handed them back to her with the grammar open at "Conjugation of Verbs." It was what the parents pronounced a "silly mess," running like this:

I love,	We love,
Thou lovest,	You love,
He loves,	They love.

Job let go of the book and ran like a deer as if to get away from his guilty self. Nancy saw him fly around the bend, and then her eyes riveted to the open book. The smitten Job had scrawled with the point of a slate pencil after the "simple declarative sentence, first person, singular number—"
"You."

Nancy blushed and her eyes snapped at an unconscious conquest as she effaced the sly confession, and went to her mother to ask if she did right to divide with Joby.

"Quite right, Nanny, but you had best not let your father know because he is having trouble with Mr. Collins."

But Nancy did tell her father, and got a scolding which did not hurt much as she was expecting a storm.

The school days of Ben and Job and their companions sped by with incidents and accidents, pleasures, disappointments, dreams and occasional hard knocks as they neared the activities of life. They fished, hunted and boated; named each rock and beach after those in which they fancied they saw a resemblance to some described in their geographies; had a hundred hairbreadth escapes from death, and surviving were the better fitted for the battles of life which all too soon fell upon their shoulders at the death of their father. Work and worry, toil and slave, was their lot before their school days should have been ended. Thus were they developed into hardy young men with a generation, who, seconding the efforts of the pioneers, have transformed a wilderness into a land smiling with peace and plenty.

The Last Haul.

"Bone Marceau, I know you didn't speak to me sence I was a kid, but here's a matter what's got to be talked about. I want yer Nancy; she wants me. I'm fair, so I promised her I'd speak if I had to do ye, ole man, but I 'low 'twon't make no great 'diff' one way or t'other."

Did ever a young man make so long and pointed a speech to a prospective father-in-law? Joby Collins was not bashful. Besides he had taken up and cherished for many years his father's grudge against old Marceau, whose characteristic reply was equally pointed:

"No; dod gast ye, no!"

The interview ended abruptly as it began. A little later in the day Ben Collins, Joby's brother, came falteringly up the lane to see old Bone on an entirely different mission.

"Good morning, Mr. Marceau," he said, "would you give us another five years on the mortgage? We can not pay more than the interest today, but if we have luck this season our fishing will give us a start."

"Ben Collins, your father injured me, and I will not accommodate one of your name. Git right offen these premises and don't let me see your face 'till you come with principal and interest, and that's the hull on't. Now go!"

Insulted and disheartened, the young man turned homeward, while his obdurate creditor shuffled down a path to the water.

It was a dull November day and old Bone, in a sullen mood, alone walked the shore of a bight in one of the Great Lakes. The water was lazily lapping the rocky ledges as the dead seas soberly followed each other shoreward from the lake as if wearied with the tossing they had received in the gale of the previous night. The whole sky was heavy with dark clouds that moved not. Sea gulls were bold in their pursuit of dead or disabled fish, and Bone noticed how distinctly the white wings flashed against the leaden sky. The dull waters gave back no reflection save here and there that of a dirty leg-of-mutton sail that in the absence of sunlight appeared almost white. The atmosphere was hazy, and the distant shore loomed above the horizon as if rising on tiptoe to see what old Bone was storming about now.

Seventy years, man and boy, he had been fisherman and sailor, and as he passed the Collins boys washing and mending their nets a pang of jealousy shot into his soul, and his heart grew heavy with his own unfitness for the activities of life. Hardship and exposure had been his lot, and now, drawn with rheumatic pains, his life of idleness was worse than a prison. He wandered slowly along the bare rocks where for years his seines had bagged loads of fish, and fell to observing the weather after the manner of those who perpetuate the habit when retired from the water.

"The herring should run the shores this day if ever," he said half to the kingfisher that rasped a daring salute as he shot into a dead pine. "Just the day, just the weather, just

SPINNING OUT THE GREAT SEINE.

everything but fish," he continued, searching the receding bottom as if to explore the depths beyond. Then his eyes lifted to the gulls.

"Great Ingens! Them birds is flockin' just like there be fish under 'em. If my eyes wuz ten years younger, so I could bleeve 'em, I'd swar ther ware a school 'o herrin' takin' soundin's out thar."

Watching the gulls which it seemed were mobilizing under a gray-backed leader, the old fisherman moved farther down the point with more animation. The noisy squawking of these garbagers of the sea reached his ears as they assembled from north, south, east and west, some seeming to drop from the very zenith. He gazed intently at the unusual demonstration.

"Fish, or wind?" he queried, as a little ripple, not unlike a cat's paw, broke the glassy surface.

"They be flockin' shoreward," he exclaimed, as the birds chased each other like snowflakes, the mass rolling over and over itself, but unmistakably heading toward shoal water. From exhaustion the old fisherman's gaze dropped downward. Then he winked hard and rubbed his eyes. Only a few feet from the shore and just under the surface a dark streak was advancing toward him, and growing bigger with every wave. It was wedge-shaped and squirming, writhing and rolling, the point suddenly turned up shore sweeping away in a graceful curve like the tail of a comet.

"Fish! Fish, sartin's my head's lookin' for'ard," he fairly shouted.

Then he started to carry the news to his neighbor fishermen, paused, then sat down. "For why," thought he, "should I tell Ben and Job Collins. If luck fails them this fall their farm's a goner. Twenty years ago their father, old Hank, cut

my seine an' I never had the fust chanst to even up fair,
Aint they beauties; millions on 'em, an' them fools don't
know's ther's a fish anigh the shore. Show! Bone, you'r grow-
in' meaner and fooler, no mistake, but thet thar Job's payin'
too stiddy attention to my Nan, and no Marceau shall marry
a Collins while I live. But she's dead set on Joby, she is, and
I'm sorry to disappint her. Tell them? In course I will,"
and he hurried to the sons of the man against whom he held
a grudge although the grave had closed between them. He
gave orders like a ship's first officer:

"Boys, ther a big school hit agin the shore! Out and
make the biggest haul ever made. Off with yer boat and run
the old 'man-killer' around shiploads on 'em."

The old man sprang into the boat and seized an oar, the
Collins boys, owners of the biggest seine on the shore, following
in dumb surprise, while those who fished for a "hand-share,"
wild with visions conjured by old Bone's excitement, grasped
the oars and sent the heavy boat around the course spinning
out the great seine as it never went before. Soon the outer
jackstaff was tossed over, a heavy rope was made fast to it and
the boat landed not far from its starting point. The seine lay
out a full three-quarters of a mile in a semi-circle, the buoys
marking the position where it lay fishing twenty feet top and
bottom. The ropes, attached to either end, were carried to
snatch blocks on the shore. With the aid of a horse at one
line and a windlass at the other the hauling of the great bag
shoreward began with a lively shout from the strong throats
of the lusty fisherman now fairly wild with excitement. The
old man who had so unceremoniously assumed command led
and cheered the men in the hard, wet task and seemed ani-
mated with the vigor of youth as the jacks dragged slowly
home. Zip! Splash! A silver streak shoots over the cork-

line and drops outside into deep water and freedom. The
fishermen have lost a fine salmon. The jacks are hove home ;
the lead-line hitches on the rough bottom ; the fish break the
surface and bag the net outward as they are drawn into smaller compass. The men tug at the lines, the corks bob under
as the finny prisoners make a frantic rush for deep water only
to be hurled back by the straining meshes. Now a long,
strong pull and all together as the jacks are landed high and
dry, and scoops are brought to land the captive beauties whose
beauty is entirely lost upon their captors. Again and again
is the net thrown until it is returned empty. Meantime the
dressers have come from up and down the shore, and each fish
is deftly prepared for market in just three moves. Frolicsome
lads and lassies they when work is over. At last the final
basket of fish has been washed and salted. Then the old fisherman who had worked with untiring energy wearily sat down
upon an overturned fish box.

"A hundred and twenty barrels," he muttered, "good
for an even thousand dollars if a cent. Never the likes of it
on this shore, never—an' I told Old Hank's boys. I do'no,
spose I may's well make a day of it. Joby, come here. You
can have Nan an' I give in. Take her for yourn an deal fair
by her."

He was pale and trembling. "Boys," he said slowly,
"its my last haul, the biggest ever made and I gin it to yer
free. Lord—help—me." And as he fell his soul went out
on that unknown deep without compass or rudder.

THE END.

www.ingramcontent.com/pod-product-compliance
Lightning Source LLC
Chambersburg PA
CBHW032116230426
43672CB00009B/1753